WORDS
AND IMAGES

WORDS
AND IMAGES

A STUDY IN THEOLOGICAL
DISCOURSE

———

E. L. MASCALL

Student of Christ Church, Oxford
University Lecturer in the
Philosophy of Religion
Priest of the Oratory of the Good Shepherd

Βλέπομεν γὰρ ἄρτι δι
ἐσόπτρου ἐν αἰνίγματι

THE RONALD PRESS COMPANY
NEW YORK

First published in Great Britain in 1957
by Longmans, Green and Co Ltd
© 1957 by E. L. Mascall

PRINTED IN GREAT BRITAIN

MAGISTRO REVERENDO

GEORGIO TIBBATTS

ORATORII BONI PASTORIS

SUPERIORI
ECCLESIAE CATHEDRALIS MASASIENSIS

CANONICO

ANIMO GRATO AMANTI

FOREWORD

CHRISTIAN philosophers have long been familiar with atheists who deny that there is a God and with agnostics who deny that we can know whether there is a God or not; and it might well appear that the problem of the existence of God was the fundamental problem of Christian philosophy. Within the last quarter of a century, however, it has become plain that there is an even more primordial question that needs to be investigated before we can even begin to inquire into the evidence for the existence of God, namely the question whether the utterances which we make when we believe ourselves to be either asserting or denying that God exists have any significance whatever. It was the great achievement of the logical positivists of the early nineteen-thirties to force this question upon the attention of apologists for theism; and, although it would be very difficult today to find anyone who held precisely the logical positivist position, the fact remains that anyone who argues for the existence of God (or, for that matter, anyone who argues against it) must be prepared to meet not only the accusation that his statements are untrue but also the accusation that they are meaningless.

It would be wrong to suppose that Christian philosophers have taken this accusation lying down, but it would be equally wrong to suppose that they have been dismayed by it. Most of them today are heartily grateful that it has forced them to make a more thorough examination than they had previously made of the status and nature of their utterances.

At their best they had always been willing and indeed anxious to admit that there was something very peculiar about theological assertions which sharply differentiated them from the assertions of ordinary conversation; and the medieval theologians had constructed a department of logic—the doctrine of analogy—expressly to deal with this fact. The medieval theologians, however, lived in the Middle Ages and more recent theologians seem to have been strangely unaware of the problem, which in any case needed for its modern discussion something more than the forms of medieval thought. Only when it was forced upon them by twentieth-century empiricists did they take it as seriously as it deserved to be taken.

Some of the results of this impact I have tried to assess in this present small book, and I have tried to write in a way which will be intelligible and perhaps even interesting to others than professional philosophers and theologians. I am solely responsible for its deficiencies, but for anything that is useful in it I am largely indebted, directly or indirectly, to the group of philosophers and theologians which, under the perhaps somewhat pretentious name of the Metaphysicals, has been meeting regularly in Oxford for almost the last ten years. If any of them are startled by unacknowledged plagiarisms they will, I am sure, be indulgent to their grateful secretary. I am only sorry that their symposium *Faith and Logic* has appeared too late for me to make detailed reference to it in the course of my discussion.

E.L.M.

CONTENTS

ACKNOWLEDGMENTS

We are indebted to the following for permission to reproduce copyright material:

Messrs. Geoffrey Bles Ltd. for an extract from *Miracles* by C. S. Lewis; Miss D. E. Collins, Messrs. Methuen & Co. Ltd., and Messrs. Dodd, Mead & Co. Inc. for an extract from "A Second Childhood" from *Collected Poems of G. K. Chesterton*, copyright 1932 by Dodd, Mead & Co. Inc.; The Dacre Press: A. & C. Black Ltd. for extracts from *The Glass of Vision* by Austin Farrer; Messrs. Gerald Duckworth & Co. Ltd. for passages from *G. F. Watts* by G. K. Chesterton; The Trustees of the Arthur Stanley Eddington Memorial Trust for extracts from *An Empiricist's View of the Nature of Religious Belief* by R. B. Braithwaite; Messrs. Faber and Faber Ltd. and Pantheon Books Inc. for extracts from *Leisure, The Basis of Culture* by Josef Pieper; Messrs. Victor Gollancz Ltd. and Dover Publications Inc., New York, for passages from *Language, Truth and Logic* by A. J. Ayer; The S. C. M. Press Ltd. and The Macmillan Company, New York, for material from *New Essays in Philosophical Theology* edited by Flew and MacIntyre, copyright 1955 by the authors; and Professor Norman Kemp Smith for an extract from his translation of Kant's *Critique of Pure Reason*, published in this country by Messrs. Macmillan & Co. Ltd. and in America by St. Martin's Press, Inc., of New York.

I

IS THEOLOGICAL DISCOURSE POSSIBLE?

1. THEOLOGY AND VERIFICATION

THERE is nothing new in the discovery that a peculiar problem is raised by the fact that human beings from time to time make utterances which purport to be statements about God, that is to say, which claim to speak about the ineffable and to describe the indescribable. There is a whole branch of traditional Christian theology—the doctrine of analogy—whose main concern is with this problem. There is, however, something new about the way in which the matter has been raised in recent years; and it is a way which, if it is valid, is highly destructive not only of Christian theism as it has usually been understood but of any religion which involves belief in a transcendent deity. Little excuse should therefore be needed for devoting some space to its discussion.

Some preliminary remarks may help to clarify the issue. In the first place, it should be observed that, although the problem of theological discourse and the problem of theological knowledge are not identical, they are very closely connected and it is practically impossible to discuss either of them without also discussing the other. Talking about God and knowing God are not necessarily identical or even co-extensive; there may be such a thing as wordless knowledge. Nevertheless we cannot talk about even wordless knowledge

I

without using words to discuss it; and our discussion of it is likely to be very unprofitable if at the same time we make no attempt to discuss its object. I shall try not to confuse the two activities, but it will be quite impossible to separate them.

Again, we must recognise that it is impossible to separate the question whether God can be talked about from the question of the kind of things that people say when they talk about him. The word 'God' must have some content if our statements about God are to be intelligible at all; and if we say what the content is we are inevitably saying things about him. We shall thus be discussing in this book not one question but a number of closely related ones; and we may note that some of the confusion in which the subject has been involved has been due to a failure to distinguish between them.

I shall begin by examining the position that was put forward by Mr. (now Professor) A. J. Ayer in 1936 in his famous little book *Language, Truth and Logic,* in spite of the fact that nobody, perhaps not even Professor Ayer himself, appears to hold exactly that position today. This seems to me to be worth while for two reasons. In the first place, there are a good many people alive whose philosophical studies ended about that date, and, since Professor Ayer's book was given something of the character of a manifesto, as the statement of a philosophy which was to end philosophising, there may still be point in making a brief reference to it, in spite of the large number of criticisms, of various degrees of penetration, which have appeared since it was published. In the second place, most of what has been written on the question in recent years has derived, either directly or indirectly, from Professor Ayer's thesis, even if only by way of reaction against it; and it is in practice almost impossible to take any other starting point for our discussion. It ought in fairness to be recognised that, ten years after its first publication, Professor Ayer added to his book a new Introduction which contained certain modifications of his original position; but how firmly entrenched that position was is shown by how few and insignificant those modifications were.

The basis of Ayer's system was the famous 'verification principle', in formulating which Ayer claimed to be simply expressing in the most clear-cut way the fundamentally empirical character of the tradition in British philosophy which derives from the great eighteenth-century Scottish philosopher David Hume. The principle had indeed been already stated in the most extreme form by philosophers of the Viennese School, in particular by M. Schlick, for whom the sole criterion of the meaningfulness of a statement was the possibility of verifying it by sense-experience. This is what Ayer called 'verifiability in the strong sense': 'A proposition is said to be verifiable, in the strong sense of the term, if, and only if, its truth could be conclusively established in experience.'[1] For Ayer, however, verifiability in the strict sense seemed to be far too drastic a criterion of meaningfulness; for it would dismiss as meaningless many statements which he was convinced were undoubtedly meaningful. It would rule out general statements, such as 'Arsenic is poisonous,' which could not be conclusively verified so long as any fragment of arsenic remained unconsumed, statements about inaccessible events and objects, such as 'There are mountains on the other side of the moon,' whose unverifiability might be overcome by a sufficient development of the science of astronautics, and also statements about the past, such as 'Napoleon was defeated at Waterloo,' which could be conclusively verified only by the impossible method of going back in time to the year

[1] *Language, Truth and Logic* (2nd ed.), p. 37.

1815 and observing what happened. Ayer therefore adopted a mitigated or 'weak' verification principle, according to which a statement is meaningful if it is possible for experience to render it *probable*; 'the question that must be asked about any putative statement of fact is not, Would any observations make its truth or falsehood logically certain? but simply, Would any observations be relevant to the determination of its truth or falsehood? And it is only if a negative answer is given to this second question that we conclude that the statement under consideration is nonsensical.'[1] Some minor modifications were made in Ayer's second edition, but they do not affect our present considerations.

For Ayer, then (and here I mean the Ayer of the two editions of *Language, Truth and Logic*), a statement which purports to be a statement of fact is genuine and meaningful if, and only if, some possible empirical observations can be specified which would be relevant to the determination of its truth or falsehood. He does, indeed, recognise that there is another kind of meaningful statements, but these are not statements of fact; they are simply tautologies, like the statement 'Either all the ants that there are are carnivorous or there is at least one ant that is not,' and they provide no information about any matter of fact whatever.

Having laid down his verification principle, Ayer then proceeds by the use of it to dismiss as meaningless and nonsensical all ethical, metaphysical and theological statements. Ethical statements emerge from the trial with a reprieve, but only with the loss of their status as statements; they survive as expressions and stimulants of feeling, or as exhortations to action. Metaphysical and theological statements, on the other hand, receive the shortest of shrift; for they claim to make factual assertions about entities which are not objects of sense-

---

[1] *Language, Truth and Logic* (2nd ed.), p. 38.

experience, and this is the unforgivable sin. 'We are often told', writes Ayer, 'that the nature of God is a mystery which transcends the human understanding. But to say that something transcends the human understanding is to say that it is unintelligible. And what is unintelligible cannot significantly be described.'[1] (I will only comment in passing on the ambiguity in the use of the word 'transcends' in the first two sentences of this quotation.) Nor will Ayer have any truck with mystical experience as anything more than a psychological phenomenon. 'The mystic, so far from producing propositions which are empirically verified, is unable to produce any intelligible propositions at all. . . . It is no use his saying that he has apprehended facts but is unable to express them. For we know that if he really had acquired any information, he would be able to express it.'[2] ('Do we?' we might interpose.) And again:

If the man who asserts that he is seeing God is merely asserting that he is experiencing a peculiar kind of sense-content, then we do not for a moment deny that his assertion may be true. But, ordinarily, the man who says that he is seeing God is saying not merely that he is experiencing a religious emotion, but also that there exists a transcendent being who is the object of this emotion; just as the man who says that he sees a yellow patch is ordinarily saying not merely that his visual sense-field contains a yellow sense-content, but also that there exists a yellow object to which the sense-content belongs. And it is not irrational to be prepared to believe a man when he asserts the existence of a yellow object, and to refuse to believe him when he asserts the existence of a transcendent God. For whereas the sentence 'There exists here a yellow-coloured material thing' expresses a genuine synthetic proposition which could be em-

[1] Ibid., p. 118. More recently Ayer has become rather more indulgent about metaphysics, but he is as hostile as ever to theology.
[2] Ibid., p. 118.

B

pirically verified, the sentence 'There exists a transcendent god' has, as we have seen, no literal significance.[1]

We are not concerned at the moment with Ayer's theory of ethical statements; we are, however, concerned with his theory of theological statements, and also with his theory of metaphysical statements in so far as theological statements are themselves metaphysical. And there are, I think, at least four important comments to be made on his use of the verification principle.

First, there is something very suspicious about the fact that the verification principle had to be mitigated. In its original 'strong' form it had all the downright simplicity that a fundamental philosophical principle might be expected to have. But, writes Ayer, 'it seems to me that if we adopt conclusive verifiability as our criterion of significance, as some positivists have proposed, our argument will prove too much'. 'Too much for what?' we might inquire, with a notion that the answer is 'Too much for Ayer.' It would be a manly, robust and, as Ayer himself says, a heroic course[2] to apply the principle ruthlessly regardless of the casualties that might result. But this would demolish many types of statement whose meaningfulness Ayer wishes to preserve, such as the statements already quoted about arsenic and the mountains on the far side of the moon and Napoleon. Why should they not be in fact demolished? Is it because Ayer has some independent criterion of significance and is trimming the verification principle to conform to it? It looks as if this is the case. But if so, why should we not trim the principle a little more in order to let in ethical, metaphysical or even (*sit venia verbis*) theological statements? Who is to decide where the line is to be drawn?

---

[1] *Language, Truth and Logic* (2nd. ed.) p. 119.   [2] Ibid., p. 37.

Secondly, what sort of statement is the verification principle itself? Ayer undoubtedly thinks it is meaningful, but it does not obviously belong to either of the two types of meaningful statement which he recognises. If he had taken the heroic course of nailing his colours to the mast of the 'strong' form of the principle, some sort of case might have been made for the point of view that the principle was a tautology, that 'meaningful' and 'empirically verifiable' were simply synonyms or at least that 'empirically verifiable' was part of the content of 'meaningful'. Even so, I think, the assertion would have been questionable, for we have, I would maintain, only to think of the phrases 'empirically verifiable' and 'meaningful' to see that they do not *mean* the same thing. Some philosophers might have held that, in spite of this difference of meaning, 'Meaningful entails empirically verifiable' was a synthetic *a priori* truth, but this way is not open to Ayer, who denies that there are such things as synthetic *a priori* truths. Is the principle, then, an empirical generalisation? That is to say, has Ayer examined a large variety of statements for meaningfulness and concluded that all those that were meaningful conformed to the principle and that all those that were meaningless did not conform to it? I have suggested that this is almost what he seems to claim to have done, in the somewhat arbitrary way in which he has mitigated the verification principle. However, in the Introduction to his second edition he denies this explicitly, when he writes as follows: 'While I wish the principle of verification itself to be regarded, not as an empirical hypothesis, but as a definition, it is not supposed to be entirely arbitrary.'[1] What, in this sentence, is the force of the statement 'it is not supposed

---

[1] Ibid., p. 16. This is repeated almost word for word in Ayer's essay on 'The Vienna Circle' in the symposium *The Revolution in Philosophy*, published in 1956 (p. 75).

to be entirely arbitrary' it is indeed difficult to see; but its introduction seems to manifest a reprehensible desire to run with the hare and hunt with the hounds. For the assertion that the principle is a definition makes it impossible to question its truth, while the assertion that it is not entirely arbitrary suggests that some ground for its assertion is to be found in experience. This dual character is, however, just what Ayer elsewhere alleges that no statement can have, and one of his chief grievances against metaphysical and theological statements is that they—or some of them—claim to have it. This assertion that the verification principle is a definition will, however, bring us to our third comment.

For, if Ayer simply defines 'meaningful' as equivalent to 'verifiable in the weak sense or else tautological', no harm is done to either metaphysical or theological statements by saying that, in *this* sense, they are meaningless or nonsensical. What would be harmful would be a demonstration that they were meaningless in the common or garden sense of 'unintelligible', and this is in fact nowhere proved. If the verification principle is simply a definition, it can assert nothing, for the function of definitions is not to make assertions but to register our linguistic conventions; if, on the other hand, it is a statement of fact, then it is a synthetic proposition, and, in virtue of the very assertion which it makes, itself needs empirical verification. Ayer seems in fact to have fallen into the snare in which the empiricists customarily claim to find the metaphysicians, that of packing into their principles the conclusions which they want to get out of them, as a conjuror inserts the rabbit into the hat before he comes on to the stage. This is the method of which Lord Russell has remarked that it has many advantages, but that they are the advantages which theft has over honest toil.[1] But in fact, in his second

[1] *Introduction to Mathematical Philosophy*, p. 71.

edition Ayer makes a number of admissions which are extremely damaging to his former thesis. Thus he admits that there may be definitions of 'meaning' according to which statements which are neither tautological nor empirically verifiable may be meaningful and that there is some proper use of the word 'understanding' according to which such statements may be capable of being understood. He adds that this will not be the sense in which scientific hypothesis or commonsense statements are understood, but I do not imagine that anyone ever thought that it was. He tells us that he would still defend the use of the criterion of verifiability as a methodological principle, but this remark as it stands is nothing more than an interesting statement of his own preferences and habits. His final admission is that for the effective elimination of metaphysics the criterion needs to be supported by detailed analyses of particular metaphysical arguments, and this is very remarkable.[1] For it reduces the verification principle to the level of a generalisation from experience, namely the experience of examining a number of metaphysical arguments, and as long as any metaphysical arguments remain unexamined (which will presumably be always the case, as their number is potentially infinite) there is always the possibility that one of them will turn out to be valid and at the same time to violate the verification principle. If one compares the bold assertions in Ayer's first edition with the somewhat tentative and hedging remarks in the relevant passages of the second, one is tempted to feel that one is witnessing a very skilful rearguard action, in which Ayer rapidly oscillates between a number of positions, treating the verification principle at one moment as a definition, at another as a truth of logic and at another as an empirically verified generalisation. To be convicted of this procedure would

[1] Op. cit., p. 16.

leave some philosophical systems unabashed, but for Ayer's it is fatal. For the absolute distinction between truths of logic and statements of empirical fact is its basic doctrine, and it is precisely for their violation of this doctrine that it condemns its competitors. Nothing could therefore be more damaging to it than the discovery that it has itself fallen into the commission, in however small a degree, of this unforgivable sin.

My fourth criticism of Ayer is that, having made the apparently innocent and plausible assertion that all meaningful assertions must have some reference to experience, he then goes on to limit the meaning of experience in the narrowest and most arbitrary way to the experience of the bodily senses. Once again, we want to know what is the logical status of this assumption. If it is alleged to be a tautology, it seems pretty clear that this allegation is false, for there is nothing logically impossible in an experience which is not an experience of sense impressions upon the physical organs of the body. If, on the other hand, it is alleged to be an empirical generalisation, there is a good deal of experience, namely mystical experience in the broadest sense, which *prima facie* contradicts it and which certainly ought not to be dismissed without detailed examination. But in Ayer's book such an examination is nowhere made. The remarks which he does pass upon mystical experience are, however, highly revealing.

> We do not deny *a priori* [he writes] that the mystic is able to discover truths by his own special methods. We wait to hear what are the propositions which embody his discoveries, in order to see whether they are verified or confuted by our empirical observations. But the mystic, so far from producing propositions which are empirically verified, is unable to produce any intelligible propositions at all. And therefore we say that his intuition has not revealed to him any facts. It is no use his saying that he has apprehended facts but is unable to express

them. For we know that if he really had acquired any information, he would be able to express it. . . . So that in describing his vision the mystic does not give us any information about the external world; he merely gives us indirect information about the condition of his own mind.[1]

Everything here turns upon the way in which the word 'empirical' has been smuggled into the second sentence of this passage. We may grant that if the mystic's language bore no relation whatever to the experience of any of his hearers or readers it could convey nothing to them. But this is not the case. The mystics do in fact use a great deal of language derived from sensory experience, the language of sight and touch and taste, while they emphasise that these words are not to be taken in their ordinary crude applications. They also at times appeal to non-sensory experiences which they assume that some at least of their hearers will have had and will be able to identify as of essentially the same type as their own. This use of language is undoubtedly odd, and it will certainly be misinterpreted by anyone who supposes that the only intelligible use of language derived from sense experience is its use in the registration of the occurrence of sense-phenomena. When Ayer waits for the mystic to enunciate propositions which are verified or confuted by empirical observations, he will certainly be disappointed. The mystic does not produce, at least as a general rule, propositions which are empirically verified, and, if he does, these will not be theological propositions. But to say that he does not produce any intelligible theological propositions at all is to make a dogma into a wall which hides the most obvious facts. Anyone who takes the trouble to study diligently the writings of the mystics can verify this for himself. Mystical theology, like other pursuits (physical science for example), has its own way of

[1] Ibid., p. 118.

talking,[1] which can be misleading or even flatly unintelligible
to the complete outsider. The way in which its language is
related to the reality with which it is concerned is as indirect
and raises at least as many problems as the language which
physical science uses to deal with the reality with which *it* is
concerned. And, unlike the subject-matter of physics, the
subject-matter of mystical theology is supremely mysterious
and needs (so its practitioners tell us) for its understanding
not merely training in a technique but purity of heart and
religious devotion. It is furthermore alleged that, in the
present life, very few persons are privileged to apprehend this
reality with full immediacy and intensity. All this is true, yet
the fact remains that the language of mystical experience,
like, on a lower level, the language of dogmatic theology, can
in fact be understood by those who are prepared to learn to
do this. That finite minds can apprehend a transcendent and
infinite reality and that human language can communicate
information about it is no doubt very surprising, but it happens to be true; and to rule the language either of dogmatic or
of mystical theology out of court, on the grounds that it fails
to conform to an externally imposed prejudice as to what
types of statement ought to be intelligible, is simply to exclude
from consideration great tracts of reality and to confine oneself within a constricted and impoverished world. In Berkeley's phrase, it is to cast dust in one's eyes and then complain that one cannot see. I shall discuss this matter in more
detail later on. At the moment I merely wish to make it
plain that I am far from asserting that all our knowledge of
God, or even the greater part of it, is derived from mystical
experience in the strict sense, that is to say from a direct
experimental awareness of God in which the senses play no
part. But I do want to point out that Ayer's denial of the

[1] Cf. p. 94 infra.

possibility of such awareness rests upon a sheer ambiguity in the use of the word 'empirical', which is used first in an extremely general sense in order to make the verification principle plausible and then in an extremely specialised sense in order to rule out all experience except that of sense-phenomena.

It is, I would maintain, clear to anyone who approaches the matter with an open mind, that the fundamental criterion of meaningfulness is not sense-verifiability but intelligibility, that is to say that in order to know whether a statement has meaning you should see whether it is possible to understand it. This statement is of course a tautology, and therein lies its strength. For meaningfulness is a primary notion, which cannot be described in terms of anything else. As Mr. J. O. Wisdom has said, 'with statements that can be understood independently of verification, to say that the verification provides the meaning is to confuse the meaning of a statement with the evidence for its truth'.[1] I am far from denying that the verification principle has a very considerable use, if a limited one, as a methodological principle. If you are uncertain whether a statement is significant or not it may be very useful to inquire what you would do in order to test its truth or falsehood. And this may involve subjecting it to the criterion of sense-verifiability. But the validity of this process depends upon its being the kind of statement to which the process is appropriate, and this can only be determined by examining it to see what kind of statement it is. I think that in fact a good many of the statements made by idealist philosophers are indefinite and confused, that they frequently fall into ambiguity and sometimes simply make mistakes in their arguments; they are not the only philosophers to go astray in these ways. But one of the difficulties in getting to grips with

[1] *The Metamorphosis of Philosophy*, p. 75.

* Ayer's strictures upon theology arises from the fact that he seems to have read very little theology, and to have a totally inadequate notion of the way that theologians think and the things that they say. This is a provocative statement, but I hope to provide justification for it in the course of this book.

2. THEOLOGY AND FALSIFICATION

The subsequent development of this debate is well illustrated by a discussion which took place at Oxford in 1950 and 1951 in the pages of a short-lived periodical called *University*; the more important contributions to it have recently been reprinted in the volume *New Essays in Philosophical Theology* edited by Professor A. G. N. Flew and Mr. Alasdair MacIntyre. The initial stimulus to this discussion was provided by a famous paper by Mr. (now Professor) John Wisdom with the title 'Gods,' which appeared in the *Proceedings of the Aristotelian Society* for 1944–5.[1] In this paper Wisdom had argued that, with the increasing tendency on the part of theists and non-theists alike to account for natural phenomena by purely natural causes, '*the existence of God is not an experimental issue in the way it was*'.[2] This does not mean that he rejected religion as necessarily pointless or foolish; he was prepared to admit that, like artistic experience, it might have very considerable psychological value. '*If we say as we did at the beginning that when a difference as to the existence of a God is not one as to future happenings then it is not experimental and therefore not as to the facts, we must not forthwith assume that there is no right and wrong about it*, no rationality or irrationality, no appropriateness or inappropriateness, no

[1] Reprinted in *Logic and Language* (First Series), edited by A. G. N. Flew, and in *Philosophy and Psychoanalysis*, by John Wisdom.
[2] *Logic and Language*, I, p. 187.

procedure which tends to settle it, *nor even that this procedure is in no sense a discovery of new facts.*' But, he said, 'the difference as to whether a God exists involves our feelings more than most scientific disputes and in this respect is more like a difference as to whether there is beauty in a thing'.[1] It is interesting to note that, in order to reach his conclusion that the existence of God is no longer, in the ordinary sense of the words, an experimental issue, Wisdom felt forced to exclude from his purview the possibility that the existence of God might be verified in the experience of life beyond the grave. 'I do not want', he wrote, 'to consider here expectations as to what one will see and feel after death nor what sort of reasons these logically unique expectations could have. So I want to consider those theists who do not believe in a future life, or rather, I want to consider the differences between atheists and theists in so far as these differences are not a matter of belief in a future life.'[2] This is a somewhat damaging qualification of Wisdom's thesis, for, although there must be very few theists who hold that we have no knowledge of God in this life and who relegate our experience of him entirely to the other world, Wisdom's attempt to reduce religion to the level of psychology remains unfulfilled so long as this possibility is still open. However, I shall not pursue this point at the moment, as our immediate concern is with his famous parable of the Invisible Gardener, which provided the starting-point of the *University* discussion. I shall state the parable in the short but accurate summary which is given by Flew in the article in which that discussion was initiated.

Once upon a time two explorers came upon a clearing in the jungle. In the clearing were growing many flowers and many weeds. One explorer says, 'Some gardener must tend this plot.'

[1] Ibid., p. 197.   [2] Ibid., p. 188.

The other disagrees, 'There is no gardener.' So they pitch their tents and set a watch. No gardener is ever seen. 'But perhaps he is an invisible gardener.' So they set up a barbed-wire fence. They electrify it. They patrol with bloodhounds. (For they remember how H. G. Wells's *The Invisible Man* could be both smelt and touched though he could not be seen.) But no shrieks ever suggest that some intruder has received a shock. No movements of the wire ever betray an invisible climber. The bloodhounds never give cry. Yet still the Believer is not convinced. 'But there is a gardener, invisible, intangible, insensible to electric shocks, a gardener who has no scent and makes no sound, a gardener who comes secretly to look after the garden which he loves.' At last the Sceptic despairs, 'But what remains of your original assertion? Just how does what you call an invisible, intangible, eternally elusive gardener differ from an imaginary gardener or even from no gardener at all?'[1]

Flew's comment upon this is that 'in this parable we can see how what starts as an assertion, that something exists or that there is some analogy between certain complexes of phenomena, may be reduced step by step to an altogether different status, to an expression perhaps of a "picture preference" . . . . A fine brash hypothesis may thus be killed by inches, the death by a thousand qualifications. And in this,' he continues, 'it seems to me, lies the peculiar danger, the endemic evil, of theological utterance.'[2] Such utterances, he tells us, as 'God has a plan,' 'God created the world,' 'God loves us as a father loves his children,' look very much like vast cosmological assertions. But, he continues, if they assert anything they must also deny its contradictory; if a form of words is really a factual assertion, there must be some state of affairs which would be incompatible with its truth. However, the utterances which theists make about God, such as

---

[1] *New Essays in Philosophical Theology*, p. 96.   [2] Ibid., p. 97.

those just quoted, are alleged by them to be compatible with any state of affairs whatever; nothing is allowed to count as evidence against them.

> Someone tells us that God loves us as a father loves his children. We are reassured. But then we see a child dying of inoperable cancer of the throat. His earthly father is driven frantic in his efforts to help, but his Heavenly Father reveals no obvious sign of concern. Some qualification is made—God's love is 'not a merely human love' or it is 'an inscrutable love', perhaps— and we realise that such sufferings are quite compatible with the truth of the assertion that 'God loves us as a father (but, of course, . . .).' We are reassured again. But then perhaps we ask: what is this assurance of God's (appropriately qualified) love worth, what is this apparent guarantee really a guarantee against? Just what would have to happen not merely (morally and wrongly) to tempt but also (logically and rightly) to en- title us to say 'God does not love us' or even 'God does not exist'?[1]

And so Flew put to the succeeding symposiasts the questions, 'What would have to occur or to have occurred to constitute for you a disproof of the love of, or of the existence of, God?'

After a skirmish between Fr. Thomas Corbishley, S.J., and Mr. Patrick Nowell-Smith on the question whether God's existence can or cannot be meaningfully asserted before it has been settled whether or not meaningful assertions can be made about his nature and activity, the discussion of Flew's thesis got under way with a reply from Mr. R. M. Hare.

Hare, having remarked that Flew, on the ground marked out by himself, seemed to be completely victorious, an- nounced that he proposed to shift his own ground by relating another parable. This is it:

[1] Ibid., p. 98.

A certain lunatic is convinced that all dons want to murder him. His friends introduce him to all the mildest and most respectable dons that they can find, and after each of them has retired, they say, 'You see he doesn't really want to murder you; he spoke to you in a most cordial manner; surely you are convinced now?' But the lunatic replies: 'Yes, but that was only his diabolical cunning; he's really plotting against me the whole time, like the rest of them: I know it I tell you.' However many kindly dons are produced, the reaction is still the same.[1]

Now, Hare commented, there is no behaviour of dons that can be enacted which the lunatic will accept as counting against his theory; and so, on Flew's test, his theory asserts nothing. Yet we should all agree that there is a difference between what the lunatic thinks about dons and what most of us think about them; and this suggests that Flew's doctrine is inadequate. Hare's way of putting this is to say that we differ from the lunatic in our respective *bliks*. 'He has an insane *blik* about dons; we have a sane one.'[2] *Bliks* are vitally important, for they determine our attitude to the world and to life; and yet they elude the normal tests of verification.

It was Hume who taught us that our whole commerce with the world depends upon our *blik* about the world; and that differences between *bliks* about the world cannot be settled by observation of what happens in the world. That was why, having performed the interesting experiment of doubting the ordinary man's *blik* about the world, and showing that no proof could be given to make us adopt one *blik* rather than another, he turned to backgammon to take his mind off the problem. . . .

The mistake [Hare continued] of the position which Flew selects for attack is to regard this kind of talk as some sort of *explanation*, as scientists are accustomed to use the word. As such, it would obviously be ludicrous. . . . But it is nevertheless

[1] *New Essays in Philosophical Theology*, p. 99.   [2] Ibid., p. 100.

true to say that, as Hume saw, without a *blik* there can be no explanation; for it is by our *bliks* that we decide what is and what is not an explanation. Suppose we believed that everything that happened, happened by pure chance. This would not of course be an assertion; for it is compatible with anything happening or not happening, and so, incidentally, is its contradictory. But if we had this belief, we should not be able to explain or predict or plan anything. Thus, although we should not be *asserting* anything different from those of a more normal belief, there would be a great difference between us; and this is the sort of difference that there is between those who really believe in God and those who really disbelieve in him.[1]

Hare's final reflection is as follows:

There is an important difference between Flew's parable and my own which we have not yet noticed. The explorers do not *mind* about their garden; they discuss it with interest, but not with concern. But my lunatic, poor fellow, minds about dons. . . . It is because I mind very much about what goes on in the garden in which I find myself, that I am unable to share the explorers' detachment.[2]

One of the most impressive features of Hare's rejoinder, as compared with Flew's original statement, is his emphasis upon the fact that theistic belief involves much more for the theist than a detached intellectual acceptance of the truth of the proposition 'God exists.' But I think Flew was right when, in summing up the debate, he remarked upon two weaknesses in Hare's position. The first was that the Christian affirmations would hardly be orthodox if given Hare's interpretation: 'if Hare's religion really is a *blik*, involving no cosmological assertions about the nature and activities of a supposed personal creator, then surely he is not a Christian at all?'[3] The second weakness was that, thus interpreted, the

[1] Ibid., p. 101.   [2] Ibid., p. 102.   [3] Ibid., p. 108.

Christian affirmations could scarcely do the job which they do. 'If they were not even intended as assertions then many religious activities would become fraudulent, or merely silly. . . . Religious utterances may indeed express false or even bogus assertions,' writes Flew, 'but I simply do not believe that they are not both intended and interpreted to be or at any rate to presuppose assertions, at least in the context of religious practice; whatever shifts may be demanded, in another context, by the exigencies of theological apologetic.'[1] I think that Flew may have been reading into Hare's exposition more than was there, although Hare is known to stand well on the logical left wing of Christian philosophy, but I would agree that his theory of *bliks* at least leaves us wondering what, if any, their factual implications are supposed to be.

No such ambiguity is discernible in the comments of Mr. B. G. Mitchell, who was perfectly clear that theistic utterances stand or fall by their claim to be assertions about the ultimate nature of things. He struck directly against Flew's accusation that the theologian allows nothing factual to be relevant to the truth or falsehood of his case. 'The theologian', he wrote, 'surely would not deny that the fact of pain counts against the assertion that God loves men. This very incompatibility generates the most intractable of theological problems—the problem of evil. So the theologian *does* recognise the fact of pain as counting against Christian doctrine. But it is true that he will not allow it—or anything—to count decisively against it; for he is committed by his faith to trust in God.'[2] And, like his predecessors, Mitchell told a parable to illustrate his point.

In time of war in an occupied country, a member of the resistance meets one night a stranger who deeply impresses him. They spend that night together in conversation. The Stranger

[1] *New Essays in Philosophical Theology*, p. 108.   [2] Ibid., p. 103.

tells the partisan that he himself is on the side of the resistance—indeed that he is in command of it, and urges the partisan to have faith in him no matter what happens. The partisan is utterly convinced at that meeting of the Stranger's sincerity and constancy and undertakes to trust him.

They never meet in conditions of intimacy again. But sometimes the Stranger is seen helping members of the resistance, and the partisan is grateful and says to his friends, 'He is on our side.'

Sometimes he is seen in the uniform of the police handing over patriots to the occupying power. On these occasions his friends murmur against him: but the partisan still says, 'He is on our side.' He still believes that, in spite of appearances, the Stranger did not deceive him. Sometimes he asks the Stranger for help and receives it. He is then thankful. Sometimes he asks and does not receive it. Then he says, 'The Stranger knows best.' Sometimes his friends, in exasperation, say 'Well, what *would* he have to do for you to admit that you were wrong and that he is not on our side?' But the partisan refuses to answer. He will not consent to put the Stranger to the test. And sometimes his friends complain, 'Well, if *that's* what you mean by his being on our side, the sooner he goes over to the other side the better.'

The partisan of the parable does not allow anything to count decisively against the proposition 'The Stranger is on our side.' This is because he has committed himself to trust the Stranger. But he of course recognises that the Stranger's ambiguous behaviour *does* count against what he believes about him. It is precisely this situation which constitutes the trial of his faith.[1]

Thus, Mitchell concluded, 'this means that I agree with Flew that theological utterances must be assertions. The partisan is making an assertion when he says "The Stranger is on our side."'[2] And he alleged that the partisan's belief is an

[1] Ibid., p. 103.   [2] Ibid., p. 105.

C

explanation: 'It explains and makes sense of the Stranger's behaviour: it helps to explain also the resistance movement in the context of which he appears. In each case it differs from the interpretation which the others put upon the same facts.'[1]

In his final summing up, Flew, while admitting Mitchell's main point (namely, that the theologian does not deny that some of the evidence counts against his belief), asserted that Mitchell's real difficulty was that he had given God attributes which rule out all possible explanations.

> In Mitchell's parable of the Stranger it is easy for the believer to find possible excuses for ambiguous behaviour; for the Stranger is a man. But suppose the Stranger is God. We cannot say that he would like to help but cannot: God is omnipotent. We cannot say that he would help if he only knew: God is omniscient. We cannot say that he is not responsible for the wickedness of others: God creates those others. . . .
>
> So [he concludes], though I entirely concede that Mitchell was absolutely right to insist against me that the theologian's first move is to look for an *explanation*, I still think that in the end, if relentlessly pursued, he will have to resort to the avoiding action of *qualification*. And there lies the danger of that death by a thousand qualifications. . . .[2]

It is perhaps relevant to note that theology is not ignorant of the problem to which Flew points in the passage last quoted. 'Either God can abolish evil and won't, in which case he isn't good, or he wants to and can't, in which case he isn't powerful' is one of the stock anti-theistic dilemmas; it was not first thought of by Flew. Theists are in fact convinced that it can be resolved without either the goodness or the power of God having to be evacuated of all significance; and they have produced elaborate arguments to prove this. Those arguments may or may not be convincing; but the

[1] *New Essays in Philosophical Theology*, p. 105.   [2] Ibid., p. 107.

reason why theologians have gone on believing that the dilemma can be resolved, whether their arguments are convincing or not, is because they have been convinced of the truth of the view which Mitchell's parable sets forth, namely, that in spite of some of the appearances, God is on our side. In fact, I think the case for Christian theism is even stronger than the parable suggests, and this for two reasons. In the first place, it is not strictly true that 'they' (that is, in the interpretation, the Christian and his God) 'never meet in conditions of intimacy again'; and secondly, Christian faith is supported, and in its first beginning was indeed generated, by a conviction to which the parable as told by Mitchell offers no parallel, that the Christian's Lord had died and risen again from the dead. That this is central to faith the New Testament bears witness: 'If Christ be not risen, then is your faith vain.'

It will be clear how far, in this discussion, the debate had moved from the simple assertion of Ayer that theological assertions were meaningless because they were not even in principle translatable into the language of sense-experience; here the complaint had been that they were formulated in such a way that any sense-experience could be held to be compatible with them. But in both cases the fundamental objection is the same, namely, that the theologian has skilfully framed his utterances in such a way that the empiricist cannot get at them, and that therefore, from the empiricist point of view, they are meaningless. It will, therefore, I think, be of considerable interest to turn to an article by Mr. I. M. Crombie on 'Theology and Falsification', which was largely inspired by the debate which we have been considering; in the volume *New Essays in Philosophical Theology* it is printed as a sequel to the symposium of Flew, Hare and Mitchell. With the first part of the article we are not here directly concerned; it inquires into the nature of the so-called arguments for the existence of God rather than into the problem of the meaningfulness of theological statements. In the second part Crombie draws attention to the fact that the use of parables—which we have seen to characterise the expositions of the three symposiasts—is in fact the method adopted by the Bible and by Christ Himself in order to communicate truth about God.

> The things we say about God are said on the authority of the words and acts of Christ, who spoke in human language, using parable; and so we too speak of God in parable—authoritative parable, authorised parable; knowing that the truth is not literally that which our parables represent, knowing therefore that now we see in a glass darkly, but trusting, because we trust the source of the parables, that in believing them and interpreting them in the light of each other, we shall not be misled, that we shall have such knowledge as we need to possess for the foundation of the religious life.'[1]

So far so good, remarks Crombie, but it is only the predicates of theological statements that are parabolic, as, for example, the word 'merciful' when we apply it to God. The subject 'God' is, however, not parabolic at all; it never occurs in any contexts other than theological ones. How then is our grasp of it to be accounted for? Here, Crombie replies, 'we are turning from revealed theology to natural theology, from the logical father to the logical mother of religious belief'.[2] Revelation, he points out, is of importance only because it is the revelation of God: 'in treating it as something important, something commanding our allegiance, we are bringing to bear upon it the category of the transcendent, of the divine'.[3] And for the nature of this category he refers back to what he

---

[1] *New Essays in Philosophical Theology*, p. 122. [2] Ibid., p. 123.
[3] Ibid., p. 123.

has said in the earlier part of his article about the sense of
contingency as the basis of belief in the existence of God.

> Such a conviction is to no extent like the conclusion of an
> argument; the sense of dependence feels not at all like being
> persuaded by arguments, but like seeing, seeing, as it were,
> through a gap in the rolling mists of argument, which alone, one
> feels, could conceal the obvious truth. One is not *persuaded* to
> believe that one is contingent; rather one feels that it is only by
> persuasion that one could ever believe anything else.[1]

Thus, Crombie urges,

> there must exist within a man's mind the contrast between the
> contingent and the necessary, the derivative and the underiva-
> tive, the finite and the infinite, the perfect and the imperfect, if
> anything is to be for him a revelation of God. Given that con-
> trast, we are given also that to which the parables or stories are
> referred. What is thus given is certainly not knowledge of the
> object to which they apply; it is something much more like a
> direction. . . . The expression 'God' is to refer to that object,
> whatever it is, and if there be one, which is such that the know-
> ledge of it would be to us knowledge of the unfamiliar term in
> the contrast between finite and infinite.
>
> Statements about God, then, are in effect parables, which are
> referred, by means of the proper name 'God', out of our
> experience in a certain direction.[2]

Having in this way decided what sort of utterances theological
statements are, Crombie then goes on to the question of their
verifiability.

> How do we stand with regard to verification and falsification?
> Must we, to preserve our claim to be making assertions, be pre-
> pared to say what would count against them? Let us see how
> far we can do so. Does anything count against the assertion

[1] Ibid., p. 113.   [2] Ibid., p. 123.

that God is merciful? Yes, suffering. Does anything count decisively against it? No, we reply, because it is true. . . .

(This, we may remember in passing, was the point which Mitchell had made in his paper.)

. . . Could anything count decisively against it? Yes, suffering which was utterly, eternally and irredeemably pointless. Can we then design a crucial experiment? No, because we can never see all of the picture. Two things at least are hidden from us; what goes on in the recesses of the personality of the sufferer, and what shall happen hereafter.[1]

Crombie admits frankly that a statement like 'God is merciful' is not verifiable in the sense of Ayer or of Flew. But, he asks, does this matter? And to answer this question he proceeds to inquire why the demand for verification or falsification is legitimate.

The demand for verifiability is, he points out, a conflation of two demands. The first is a *logical* stipulation; nothing can be a statement of fact if the notion of testing it is precluded by correctly interpreting it, that is if it is untestable in virtue of a rule of language. The second is a *communicational* stipulation; no one can understand a statement unless *he* has a fair idea how a situation about which it was true would differ from one about which it was false. And Crombie examines religious utterances from both these points of view. Such an utterance as 'God is loving' is, he points out not untestable in the former or logical sense. Christians and others agree that there is a *prima facie* incompatibility between the love of God and suffering; they differ as to whether it is only *prima facie* or not. The issue cannot be decided, but this is simply because our experience is limited. 'We cannot get into position to decide it, any more than we can get into position to

[1] *New Essays in Philosophical Theology*, p. 124.

decide what Julius Caesar had for breakfast before he crossed the Rubicon.' Crombie amusingly adds that 'for the Christian the operation of getting into position to decide it is called dying; and, though we can all do that, we cannot return to report what we find'.[1] (We may remember that Wisdom, in his essay on 'Gods' deliberately excluded from discussion the possibility that theological utterances might be verified in a future life; but he was not as clear as Crombie as to what that exclusion involved.) By this test, then, Crombie concludes, the *logical* classification of religious utterances is that of statements of fact.

With regard to the second stipulation, he admits that the matter is complicated. Within the parable, he says, we know what 'God is loving' means and how to test it; it is like testing 'My father loves me.' But, outside the parable (that is, in applying the utterance to life and the world as a whole), 'we do not know what the situation about which our parable is being told is like; we should only know if we could know God, and know even as also we have been known; see, that is, the unfolding of the divine purposes in their entirety. Such ignorance is what we ought to expect. . . . In talking we remain within the parable, and so our statements communicate; we do not know how the parable applies, but we believe that it does apply, and that we shall one day see how.'[2]

Crombie faces frankly the objection of the atheist that, if the love of God means the sort of thing that human beings experience in this life it would be better to call it by some other name. 'If being loved by God is what we experience all the time, then it is not like being loved by man; it is like being let down right and left. And in the face of so great a discrepancy, we cannot believe that God loves us, if that is supposed to be in any sense a statement of sober fact.' He

[1] Ibid., p. 126. [2] Ibid., p. 127.

admits that this objection involves the whole problem of religion. But, he replies,

> the Christian does not attempt to evade it either by helter-skelter flight, or by impudent bluff. He has his prepared positions on to which he retreats; and he knows that if these positions are taken, then he must surrender. He does not believe that they can be taken, but that is another matter. There are three main fortresses behind which he goes. For, *first*, he looks for the resurrection of the dead, and the life of the world to come; he believes, that is, that we do not see all of the picture, and that the parts which we do not see are precisely the parts which determine the design of the whole. . . . *Second*, he claims that he sees in Christ the verification, and to some extent also the specification, of the divine love. . . . *Third*, he claims that in the religious life, of others, if not as yet in his own, the divine love may be encountered. . . .[1]

And his final word is that 'religion has indeed its problems; but it is useless to consider them outside their religious context'.[2] With this I heartily agree; and it is difficult not to feel that Flew, for all his undoubted moral seriousness, is extraordinarily unaware of the way in which the believer experiences and deals with the obstacles to his belief. This, however, is a point to which I shall return later on.

[1] *New Essays in Philosophical Theology*, p. 129.   [2] Ibid., p. 130.

II

THE SENSES AND THE INTELLECT

1. THE NATURE OF SENSE-EXPERIENCE

THE two attitudes to theological discourse which were criticised in the first chapter are typical of an outlook which is prominent, and indeed predominant, in Anglo-Saxon philosophy today. For this outlook there are only two types of knowledge of which the human mind is capable, two types of truth of which it can be aware and, in consequence, two types of statement which can be significant and intelligible. There is knowledge about sense-objects and there is knowledge about the truths of logic; corresponding to these respectively there are empirically testable propositions and there are tautologies. This outlook derives of course from the famous eighteenth-century philosopher David Hume; Ayer explicitly admits this when he quotes with approval one of Hume's most celebrated rhetorical passages.

> If we take in our hand any volume; of divinity, or school metaphysics, for instance; let us ask, Does it contain any abstract reasoning concerning quantity or number? No. Does it contain any experimental reasoning concerning matter of fact and existence? No. Commit it then to the flames. For it can contain nothing but sophistry and illusion.[1]

[1] *Enquiry concerning Human Understanding*, XII, iii, cit. *Language, Truth and Logic*, 2nd ed., p. 54.

It is this assumption that I wish to question, but I must make it plain at the outset that in so doing I am not pleading in defence of idealism, either of the absolutist or of any other kind. I do not admit that the only alternative to idealism is an empiricism of the type which limits our knowledge of reality to the registration of sense-objects, and I would defend a doctrine of perception which, while every bit as empirical as Ayer's, in the sense that it asserts that all the knowledge that we can have of reality is based upon our personal experience, refuses to limit experiences to sense-experiences or to limit sense-experiences to the mere awareness of sense-phenomena.

It is perhaps worth while emphasising this repudiation of idealism, for in spite of the consistent witness of the central tradition of Christian philosophy, it is apparently widely believed that religion, including the Christian Religion, has a peculiar interest in deriving truths of fact from purely logical premises; and the frequent remonstrances of Christian philosophers against this assumption seem to be ignored as frivolous or insincere. Thus, for example, Professor C. D. Broad in an article published in 1939[1] took it for granted that the cosmological argument for the existence of God was based upon the assertion that there are some intrinsically necessary existential propositions and, in spite of the disclaimers which his article provoked, he reprinted it unaltered and without comment in a book of essays fourteen years later.[2]

There are in fact three criticisms which may be made of the type of anti-theologicism which is represented by Professor Ayer, and none of them makes any concessions to idealism; none of them attempts to deduce the proposition 'God exists'

---

[1] *Journal of Theological Studies*, XL, pp. 25 f (1939).
[2] *Religion, Philosophy and Psychical Research.* My own criticisms of this article will be found in *He Who Is*, ch. vi.

from purely logical premises. The first criticism is that sense-experience itself may consist of something more than the experience of sense-objects. The second is that experience may consist of something more than sense-experience. And the third is that there may be experience which is not expressible in sentences at all, or which is expressible only in sentences of a very peculiar kind.

To pass then, to the first criticism, we may conveniently begin at the end of the seventeenth century with the impressive figure of John Locke. For Locke, our perception of the external world consists simply of sensation, of immediate awareness of what later philosophers would call sense-impressions, sensible phenomena or sense-data, and of nothing more. It is true that Locke held that on the basis of this sensation we can, by a subsequent or even a simultaneous inference, form the idea of a real substance as its basis and its cause, but for him this inference was distinct from the act of perception and was in no way included in it. Perception was simply sensation, and therefore when Locke asked himself what the qualities of the substance were he could only answer that they were sensible qualities. Admittedly, not all sensible qualities could be attributed to the substance; the so-called secondary qualities had to be eliminated, since the substance manifested different secondary qualities to different percipients. But nothing *except* sensible qualities could be attributed to the substance; for what can you *infer* from a sense-datum except the sense-datum itself? Thus, for Locke, the real world consisted of a washed-out replica of the world of the senses, a world from which all the secondary qualities —all the colours, and sounds and smells—had vanished and only the grimly scientific primary qualities of 'bulk, number, figure and motion' remained. That Locke's doctrine was highly congenial to the scientific mind of the time is not surprising, for the primarily qualities with which he left the real world were precisely the qualities with which Newtonian mechanics—based as it was upon Newton's three laws of motion and his law of universal gravitation—was equipped to deal. In E. A. Burtt's words:

> The world that people had thought themselves living in—a world rich with colour and sound, redolent with fragrance, filled with gladness, love and beauty, speaking everywhere of purposive harmony and creative ideals—was crowded now into minute corners in the brains of scattered organic beings. The really important world outside was a world hard, cold, colourless, silent, and dead; a world of quantity, a world of mathematically computable motions in mechanical regularity.[1]

Burtt is speaking in this passage of the world of Newtonian physics, but it is every bit as true of the world of Locke's philosophy; for they are the same world.

How vulnerable Locke's doctrine proved to be is well known. For him the trans-sensory object was an inference from the sensory object; it had such qualities of the sensory object as do not depend on its being sensed—the primary qualities, but not the secondary ones. The next step was taken by Berkeley, who showed that, if Locke's view of the perceptive act is true, all the qualities of the sensory object are secondary ones and so the trans-sensory substance collapses, for there are no qualities left for it to have. We might expect that Berkeley would have drawn the conclusion that Locke's view of the perceptive act was wrong, but he was far too much a child of his age for that. What he did conclude was that there are no trans-sensory substances, and the only way in which he could continue to believe in a world whose existence is independent of our sensing it was by postulating

[1] *The Metaphysical Foundations of Modern Physical Science,* p. 236.

that there is someone who is always sensing it, namely God. The difficulties to which this postulate gave rise are well known; in particular it was never clear whether, in Berkeley's view, the objects which we sense are a selection from the objects which God senses or are only a set of objects which resemble them without being identical with them. In any case, Berkeley's doctrine proved in the end to be no more stable than Locke's, and it was left for 'that notorious atheist David Hume' to eliminate the trans-sensory substances and God together. Kant made a desperate attempt to restore the trans-sensory substance, but in vain. For his theory of the categories, in spite of its elaboration, fails as much as Hume's to extend our knowledge beyond the phenomena; and it is a commonplace among philosophers that Kant's inaccessible *noumenon* or 'thing-in-itself' is one of the most indigestible elements in his system.

Now, as I have already indicated, I wish to call in question the basic assumption upon which the whole of the movement of thought which I have just outlined depends. That assumption consists of two parts. The first part assumes that in sense-experience the perceptive element consists simply of sensation, of the registration of a sensible particular, whether that be known as a sense-datum, as a sense-object, as a phenomenon, or by some other term. The second part assumes that any activity of the intellect which is involved can only consist of a process of *inference* (which may or may not be valid) and which, taking the sensible particular as its starting-point, either *deduces* from it the existence of some inapprehensible substance as its cause, or *interprets* it as one of the components of a physical object. That is to say, perception, in the strict sense of direct awareness of a real object, is simply identified with sensation; the intellect in no way *apprehends*, it merely *infers*.

Now against this assumption I wish to put forward the view, which has a very reputable ancestry though its existence has been ignored by most modern philosophers, that the non-sensory or intellectual element in perception does not consist simply of inference, but of apprehension. According to this view, there is (at any rate normally, for we are not at the moment concerned with mystical experience) no perception without sensation, but the sensible particular (the sense-object or sense-datum or, as the scholastics would say, the sensible species) is not the terminus of perception, not the *objectum quod*, to use another scholastic phrase, but the *objectum quo*, through which the intellect grasps, in a direct but mediate activity, the intelligible extramental reality, which is the *real thing*.

It is important to distinguish this doctrine from others which superficially resemble it, for some of these others are extremely vulnerable. In particular, it has little or nothing in common with the view of Locke. For Locke, the characteristics of the real world, were all of them sensible characteristics; they were in fact primary qualities. It was admittedly a bleached and attenuated version of the world of our experience, for it had no secondary qualities; but the qualities which it had were undoubtedly sensible ones. It had no colour, smell or taste, but it had solidity, shape and extension; and the solidity, shape and extension which it had were those very qualities as our senses perceive them. (Locke does, of course, devote a good deal of space to discussing how we form the ideas of substances, but it is clear from his discussion that he is very uncertain whether there are in fact any substances corresponding to these ideas.) The real world is thus composed of a sub-set of the elements which compose the sensory world; take away from the sensory world all the secondary qualities, and the real world is what remains.

Hence, when Berkeley showed that all the sense-qualities were secondary qualities, the world became entirely subjective, and the way was open to the sceptical empiricism of Hume.

Very different is the state of affairs on the view which I am supporting. We can readily admit that all sensible qualities are subjective—are secondary qualities, in Locke's sense—but the real world remains; for, although it is perceived and known *through* our sense-experience, its contents are intelligible beings which are not sensed by the senses but apprehended by the intellect. (This, we may remark in passing, is why the physical sciences are so dominated by mathematics, for it is the intelligible and not the sensible characteristics of an object with which mathematics is concerned. Hence, for example, the same body of mathematical theory can deal with gravitational theory, electrostatics and the hydrodynamics of a non-viscous fluid; for, in spite of their differences from the point of view of sense-experience, these phenomena have, broadly speaking, the same intelligible structure and form.) Berkeley was entirely right in maintaining, against Locke, that all sensible qualities are subjective; but he was wrong in supposing that the world has no qualities except sensible ones. It is, in fact, very amusing to see the precise point in his *Three Dialogues between Hylas and Philonous* at which this supposition is slipped in. Hylas has been granted permission to restate his case and correct any oversights of which he may have been guilty. 'One great oversight,' he said, 'I take to be this: that I did not sufficiently distinguish the *object* from the *sensation*. Now though this latter may not exist without the mind, yet it will not thence follow that the former cannot.' 'What object do you mean?' rejoins Philonous, 'The object of the senses?' 'The same,'[1] replies Hylas, and

[1] *Dialogues*, I (Everyman edition, p. 226).

plays straight into Philonous's hands. Before he knows where he is he has been made to admit that the sensible qualities of the tulip which he sees—its redness, its yellowness and so forth—cannot exist except in a perceiving mind. But if in reply to Philonous's question he had replied 'No, Philonous, not the object of the senses but the object of the intellect, which I apprehend *through* the object of the senses,' the rest of Philonous's argument would have collapsed. The misfortune of Hylas was that he was Locke in disguise; he would have fared better had he been St. Thomas Aquinas.

However, if the view that I am defending is not that of Locke, neither is it that of Kant. The intelligible object of which I have spoken is not Kant's *noumenon* or *Ding-an-sich*. For Kant, no less than for Locke, perception is reduced to sensation, but, whereas for Locke, the sense-object is an impression passively received by the mind, for Kant it has been worked up by the mind in accordance with the categories of the understanding, in order for the mind to have something which it can perceive. It is thus even more difficult for Kant than for Locke to get beyond the subjective sense-impression to a real intelligible object. This, however, does not prevent him from trying to get beyond it, and he is thus led to formulate the extremely difficult and unclear doctrine of the *noumenon* which, although it lies outside the sensible sphere, is nevertheless in some way apprehended by intuition. 'The understanding,' he writes,

is well aware that in viewing things in this manner, as thus apart from our mode of intuition, it cannot make any use of the categories. For the categories have meaning only in relation to the unity of intuition in space and time. . . . If, therefore, we should attempt to apply the categories to objects which are not viewed as being appearances [i.e. phenomena], we should have to postulate an intuition other than the sensible. . . . Since, however, such a type of intuition, intellectual intuition, forms no part whatsoever of our faculty of knowledge, it follows that the employment of the categories can never extend further than to the objects of experience. Doubtless, indeed, there are intelligible entities corresponding to the sensible entities; there may also be intelligible entities to which our sensible faculty of intuition has no relation whatsoever; but our concepts of understanding, being mere forms of thought for our sensible intuition, could not in the least apply to them.

Again,

the concept of a *noumenon*—that is, of a thing which is not to be thought as object of the senses but as a thing in itself, solely through a pure understanding—is not in any way contradictory. For we cannot assert of sensibility that it is the sole possible kind of intuition. . . . But none the less we are unable to comprehend how such *noumena* can be possible, and the domain that lies out beyond the sphere of appearances is for us empty. That is to say, we have an understanding which *problematically* extends further, but we have no intuition, indeed not even the concept of a possible intuition, through which objects outside the field of sensibility can be given, and through which the understanding can be employed *assertorically* beyond that field.[1]

'How near and yet how far!' we reflect on reading this passage, as we see Kant vainly striving to break the chains with which he has shackled himself. He has recognised that there is nothing contrary to logic in things existing which we cannot perceive (in this he is in advance of Professor Ayer's *Language, Truth and Logic*), and he admits that it is at least likely that, if the mind works up its objects into an intelligible form in order to be able to understand them, it has to have something to work up. But, just because, in his view, it is only the worked-up object that the mind can understand, the

[1] *Critique of Pure Reason*, trans. N. Kemp Smith (ed. 1933), pp. 268 f., 271 f.

D

unworked-up material is unintelligible. So he is forced into quite remarkable gymnastics in his attempt to understand what cannot be understood—and, let us note, what cannot be understood not because it is unfamiliar or too august for our finite intelligences but because, not having been worked up, it is inherently unintelligible. In the view which I am supporting, on the other hand, the trans-sensory object—the *noumenon*, to adopt Kant's term—is fundamentally intelligible, and we do in fact apprehend it. But the sense-object— Kant's intelligible *phenomenon*—is, in our view, *not* intelligible, except in so far as it may subsequently be made the object of a reflective act. Its function is to be sensed, not to be understood; and also to be the medium through which the intellect apprehends the intelligible object of which it is a manifestation.

In case it should be supposed that this view is artificial or sophisticated, I should wish to maintain that, although its exposition as a philosophical doctrine involves certain technicalities, it is in fact the expression of a thoroughly common-sense attitude. For the plain man is convinced that he experiences a world of things that exist independently of himself, and yet that things are not as they appear to his senses. He is never the naïve realist that some philosophers suppose him to be; he believes that the tulip that he sees 'really exists', while he is perfectly aware that its colour, apparent size, and the like, depend upon the circumstances under which he sees it. Nor does this doctrine that the intellect apprehends the intelligible object through the sense-impression, involve that the intellect is infallible in its apprehension; it can perfectly well make mistakes, and, since the medium of its knowledge is the sense-impression, the sense-impression may sometimes mislead it. The mottled leaf may be apprehended as a lizard, but this does not mean that some unusual kind of lizard—an imaginary lizard—has been apprehended; it simply means that the apprehension has been imperfect and erroneous. There never was a lizard there; we merely 'thought there was.' And, so far as epistemology is concerned, whatever may be the case as regards ophthalmics and psychology, that is all there is to say about it.

It will be obvious to some readers that the doctrine of perception which I have put forward is, broadly speaking, that of the Thomist-Aristotelian tradition. I do not think that ought to count against it. For, although it is commonly supposed that Thomist epistemology, like Thomist metaphysics, has been demolished by the modern empiricists, I do not think that is the case. The common belief that it has, is, I believe, due to an assumption, the falsity of which I hope I have already shown, that all medievals were crude realists (in the modern, and not the medieval, sense of the word). I think, however, that there are certain points in which the present doctrine goes beyond the Thomists, even if it does not certainly contradict them. For example, although St. Thomas seems to me to have been perfectly clear that the real world is a world of intelligible and not of sensible characteristics, I doubt if it ever occurred to him that this real intelligible world might not be structurally isomorphic with the world of sensible phenomena, that is to say that the entities of which it is composed may be related in a very different way from that in which sensible objects are related. In particular, I do not suppose he ever entertained the possibility that it might not have the same spatio-temporal structure or conform to the same laws of continuity as the realm of our sensible experience. Professors Toulmin and Braithwaite have recently expounded at length[1] the view that

[1] S. Toulmin, *The Philosophy of Science*; R. B. Braithwaite, *Scientific Explanation*. Cf. my *Christian Theology and Natural Science*, ch. ii.

scientific theories are 'maps' or 'models' which, by the application of the appropriate rules of interpretation, can be made to yield statements whose truth or falsehood is testable by sense-experience; I should want to go further than this and say that, while this is perfectly true, they are also statements about the constitution of the real intelligible universe. The view that scientific theories are direct assertions about the universe was, of course, common throughout the last two centuries; it was reluctantly abandoned when it was discovered that, while the universe which the senses observed went on being, for the most part, a causally governed continuous world in which space and time were distinct, the world of scientific theory became more and more unlike it, as relativity merged the concepts of space and time, and quantum theory discarded, or at least radically reconstructed, the notions of continuity and causality. Now I do not myself think that the older scientists were wrong in supposing that their theories were statements about the real world, though I do think they were wrong in assuming the real world to be a world of sensible, rather than of intelligible, objects. Nor do I think that Toulmin and Braithwaite are wrong in denying that scientific theories are direct statements about sensible objects, but I do think they are wrong in supposing that, if scientific theories are not direct statements about sensible objects, they cannot be statements about the real world at all but only formulae in a calculus from which statements about the real world can be derived. In fact, I would suggest that Toulmin and Braithwaite have fallen into the same trap as the older scientists; they have assumed, with them, that the real world is a world of sensible objects, though they differ from them radically about the way in which scientific theories refer to this world. If it is of the essence of reality to be not sensible but intelligible (even if certain vast tracts of reality are intelligible to us only through the experience of our senses), then Toulmin and Braithwaite's admirable demonstrations of the way in which scientific theories make us understand the world provide a powerful indication that scientific theories are statements about it. The key point is that the real intelligible world need not be isomorphic with the subjective sensible one. If we try to interpret the statements of relativity or the quantum theory as statements about the world of sensible phenomena we shall be driven from one nightmare to another and shall finally abandon the task in despair. And then, if we believe that the world of sensible phenomena is the real world, we shall say that scientific statements are not about the real world at all. If, however, we believe that the real world is an intelligible world with a structure different from that of the world of sensible phenomena, we shall see the statements of relativity and quantum theory as expressions of the kind of intelligibility that the real world has. We shall still need rules to guide us back to the world of sense when we verify our theories in the laboratory, and the function of those rules, if not their nature, will be very much as Toulmin and Braithwaite describe it. From the point of view of scientific methodology their discussions seem to me to be perfectly sound and exceedingly valuable. The question may therefore be asked what has been the point of all this talk about an intelligible universe and about the sense-object as the *objectum quo* of perception. The answer to that is that scientific methodology, for all its importance, is not the whole duty of man, nor indeed is it the question in which we are chiefly interested here. To develop the consequences of this assertion will be the business of a subsequent chapter, wherein we shall see in addition what are its consequences for theological discourse and argumentation. I shall now pass on to my second criticism of the anti-theologists, which is that experience may well consist of something more than sense-experience.

2. THE POSSIBILITY OF MYSTICAL KNOWLEDGE

The assertion that it is possible for human beings—or at least for some human beings—to have an immediate apprehension of a reality or realities which is not meditated by sense-experience is common to all religious systems which find a place for mysticism. Different religions, or different schools within the same religion, may differ about the frequency of this mystical apprehension, the conditions of its achievement, the desirability of trying to achieve it and, above all, about the nature of its object. The central tradition of Christendom has for the most part looked upon it as something beyond man's normal powers of attainment in this life, even under the assistance of sanctifying grace, and has considered it as a rare and unpredictable gift of an extraordinary kind, which is in no way necessary for the achievement even of the highest levels of sanctity, and which when it is given is a kind of anticipation of the beatific vision which for the time being more or less suspends the normal activities of earthly life. (This mystical contemplation of God is, of course, something quite different from the 'acquired contemplation' which a large and influential school of ascetic theologians considers to be the normal consequence of sanctifying grace in the life of prayer.) Thus St. Thomas Aquinas denies categorically that 'anyone in this life can see God in his essence' (*videre Deum per essentiam*),[1] making exceptions only, on the grounds of Scripture, for Moses and St. Paul, to whom he considers was granted a transient gift of that 'light of glory' whose permanent enjoyment is the privilege of the

---

[1] *S. Theol.*, I, xii, 11. Cf. *S.c.G.*, III, xlvii.

blessed in heaven alone.[1] (Dom John Chapman has amusingly remarked that some Benedictines have added St. Bene-
dict, and some Carmelites their traditional founder, the
prophet Elijah, to the two Biblical saints.[2]) However, it has
been generally held by Catholic mystical theologians that,
between the knowledge of God through His creatures and
the knowledge of God by his essence in the beatific vision,
there is also a direct knowledge of God 'by infused species'
which occurs in the highest mystical states.[3] We are not concerned here with the intricate discussions in which theologians have been drawn about the nature and conditions of
the mystical experience.[4] All I want to emphasise is that a
very impressive body of religious thought has affirmed the
possibility, and indeed the occurrence, of a cognitive experience which is not meditated by the senses; it is notable that a
very common phrase which is used by Catholic theologians
to describe it is 'an experimental awareness of God'. Now,
on the strictest verificationist principles it is difficult to see
why the possibility of such experience should be ruled out;
indeed to judge from their assertions about the immediacy
and compulsiveness of their awareness of the divine reality,
the mystics might almost be described as the strictest verificationists that there are.

There are, of course, considerable problems involved in
the attempt to relate the mystical experience to common
experience or to describe it in sensible terms; no one has emphasised this point more than the mystics themselves. The
problem arises in fact in two stages. It arises, first, when the
mystic, having emerged from his rapture, tries to think of it

[1] S. Theol., II, II, clxxv, 3.
[2] Encycl. of Religion and Ethics, IX, p. 96, s.v. 'Mysticism, Christian,
Roman Catholic.' [3] Cf. Chapman, loc. cit.
[4] Cf. e.g. J. Maritain, Distinguer pour unir, part ii; J. de Guibert The,
Theology of the Spiritual Life, p. 305 f.

in terms of his normal experience. As Chapman points out, following St. Thomas, the human intellect, just because of its union with the body and of the fact that its normal mode of knowledge is by means of the senses, always turns to sense-images, even when it is considering the most exalted spiritual realities (*mens convertit se ad phantasmata* is a stock Thomist tag); and in doing this it may easily fall into error.[1] And the second stage of the problem arises when the mystic, having formulated the experience to his own mind as well as he can, tries to describe it to someone else who in all probability has never had a mystical experience at all. I shall have something to say about this problem later on. At the moment, however, I am merely concerned to make two points. The first is that, surprising as it may seem, it *is* possible to describe and to discuss mystical experience; and that in consequence the doctrine of the verificationists about the relation of language to the objects which it describes is inadequate. My second point is that, even if it was indescribable in terms of normal experience and so was incapable of communication to non-mystics, mystical experience might nevertheless be perfectly genuine experience and mystics might elaborate a language for talking about it to one another. They would then be like an élite of people with sight living in a country of the blind; their less-gifted hearers would be unable to recognise the objects about which the mystics spoke to one another, though they could, by studying the way in which they talked, gather a good deal of information about the way the objects were related. The structure of the divine world might be thus understood by the non-mystic, even if its contents were hidden from him. To some extent this illustration does, I think, describe the situation in which the non-mystic who studies mysticism finds himself, but to some extent only. For part of

[1] Op. cit., pp. 95–6.

the problem which the writings of the mystics present to the philosopher arises from the fact that the mystics obstinately refuse to talk in a private language of their own, but insist upon using the words, and frequently quite commonplace and gross words, of sense-experience, upon describing the divine reality by words like 'fire' and 'light' and 'sweetness'. Partly no doubt this is due to the way in which their own minds have spontaneously turned to sensible images, *ad phantasmata*; partly no doubt it is due to their desire to share the fruits of their experience with others. The problems, linguistic, logical and epistomological, which are involved are admittedly extremely baffling. But neither the difficulty of the subject nor its refusal to conform to the requirements of sense-empiricists ought to blind us to the fact that the utterances of the mystics are not entirely unintelligible, and that they are not adequately diagnosed as merely material for morbid psychology. Still less have we any ground for denying that the mystics have a genuine cognitive experience of realities which are not cognised in sense-experience. Even if the experience was entirely incommunicable we should have no right to say that; we should only have the right to say that we knew nothing about it. This is the third objection which I have against the positions of Ayer and Flew; but it is obviously of less importance than the other two, as there is nothing much that one can say about it. In Wittgenstein's famous phrase, 'whereof one cannot speak, thereof must one be silent'.[1]

---

[1] *Wovon man nicht sprechen kann, darüber muss man schweigen.* (*Tractatus Logico-Philosophicus*, pp. 188, 189.)

III

THEISM WITHOUT GOD

1. SYMBOLISM AND BELIEF

THERE is nothing very new in the position that theological utterances cannot be taken as straightforward
factual assertions, but must, if they are to be significant, be reinterpreted in some non-natural or 'Pickwickian' sense. H. L. Mansel's famous Bampton Lectures of 1858
on the Limits of Religious Thought provide a notable
example of this. So does the 'symbolo-fideism' which was
taught in Paris in the latter part of the nineteenth century by
Auguste Sabatier and Eugène Ménégoz, with its insistence
that our images, figures and symbols of God are essentially
anthropomorphic and cannot adequately represent a transcendent being. 'These symbols', wrote Ménégoz,

> are without doubt the expression of a living reality, but the
> conformation of our brain is such that it cannot grasp that
> reality naked; our mind can apprehend it only when it presents
> itself in the garment of a more or less sensuous representation.
> . . . The task of the theologian is to lay bare the eternal truth
> from under its contingent manifestations and its historical
> formulae; moreover these formulae are subject to the laws of
> historical evolution.[1]

It may be doubted whether the symbolo-fideists recognised

[1] *Encycl. of Religion and Ethics*, XII, p. 151, s.v. 'Symbolo-fideism.'

sufficiently that, on their own principles, the expressions which they gave to the eternal truth when they had laid it bare from under its contingent manifestations and its historical formulae would themselves necessarily partake of a symbolic and relative character. There can, however, be no doubt of the widespread influence of this attitude, which may have been in some measure due to the general ignorance on the part of philosophers at the time of the fact that they were not the first people to whom the point in question had ever occurred and that a very persistent attempt had been made to deal with it in the later Middle Ages in the doctrine of analogical predication. The symbolist attitude appeared in a slightly different form in the early years of the present century in one of the strands of that complex movement Roman Catholic Modernism; two of the propositions condemned by the decree *Lamentabili* in 1907 are that 'the dogmas which the Church gives out as revealed are . . . an interpretation of religious facts, which the human mind has acquired by religious efforts' and that 'the dogmas of faith are to be held only according to their practical sense, that is, as binding rules of conduct, but not as norms of belief'.[1] What is notable in all these cases is that the rejection of theological assertions as factual statements goes not, as is commonly the case, with a repudiation of Christianity and the Christian Church, but with a fervent conviction that only by such reinterpretation as is alleged to be necessary can Christianity and the Christian Church be defended. Mansel was a devoted Anglican, the symbolo-fideists were devoted Protestants, the modernists— at least in their earlier phases—were equally devoted Roman Catholics.

It is only fair to add that in some writings which manifest this tendency the reason seems to be not that the writers personally believed that factual assertions about God and the

[1] Propositions 22, 26 (Denzinger, *Enchiridion*, 2022, 2026).

Christian mysteries were really impossible, but that they felt bound to pay lip-service to a philosophical and linguistic technique which ruled such assertions out. Thus, for example in 1917 a distinguished Anglo-Catholic lay philosopher wrote the following sentence:

> When we say there is a personal God, we merely mean that we affirm a less inadequate account of the totality of experience by asserting that there is a Being who has the experience of being God, or the experience which that phrase suggests to us, than if we deny that statement or fail to make it.[1]

Surely, the startled reader will feel, noting particularly the force of the word 'merely' in this sentence, symbolo-fideism could hardly go further than this. Nevertheless a careful study of the context in which it occurs shows that what the writer was really concerned to maintain was not that significant statements cannot be made about God, but that peculiar problems are involved in making such statements and that any knowledge that we can have of God or of anything else must in some way or another be given to us in our experience.

It is, however, possible to find one interpretation of the Christian religion, held by a philosopher whose personal profession of Christianity is of the most explicit and enthusiastic type, which denies not only that statements about God and the Christian mysteries are in any sense factual assertions but also that Christianity is bound up with the truth of any factual assertions whatever. This is the interpretation which was set out by Professor R. B. Braithwaite in his Eddington Memorial Lecture of 1955 entitled *An Empiricist's View of the Nature of Religious Belief.*

[1] W. Spens, *Belief and Practice*, p. 51.

2. Professor Braithwaite's Empirical Religion

Braithwaite takes as his starting point the verification principle in its original logical positivist form—that the meaning of a statement is given by its method of verification. In accordance with this, he divides significant statements into three types: (a) statements about particular matters of empirical fact, (b) scientific hypotheses and other general empirical statements, and (c) the logically necessary statements of logic and mathematics (and their contradictories). The first two of these are of course what many logical positivists would lump together in one class as empirical assertions. Braithwaite has no difficulty in showing that religious statements fail to stand up to the requirements of the verification principle in this form. He goes on, however, to condemn this form as too rigorous, for, he asserts, 'though a tough-minded logical positivist might be prepared to say that all religious statements are sound and fury, signifying nothing, he can hardly say that of all moral statements. For moral statements have a use in guiding conduct; and if they have a use they surely have a meaning—in some sense of meaning.'[1] Braithwaite thus follows the empiricists of the late 1930s in extending the word 'meaning' to cover wider uses than the use of mere factual verification. He substitutes for the 'verification principle' the 'use principle', that 'the meaning of any statement is given by the way in which it is used',[2] and he somewhat anxiously assures us that in doing this he is guilty of no desertion from the spirit of empiricism. 'The only way of discovering how a statement is used,' he tells us, 'is by an empirical inquiry; a statement need not itself be empirically verifiable, but that it is used in a particular way is always a straightforwardly empirical proposition.'[3]

[1] Op. cit., p. 10.   [2] Ibid.   [3] Ibid., p. 11.

On reading the sentence just quoted we might be pardoned for supposing that the way was now open for meaningfulness to be accorded to the most unblushingly 'metaphysical' utterances, but Braithwaite shows no signs of exploring this possibility. Its point is simply to let into the privileged circle moral assertions, for it is to moral assertions that the assertions of religion are to be reduced. Braithwaite in fact makes no attempt to demonstrate that metaphysical statements (and therefore theological statements interpreted metaphysically) are ruled out by the use principle as meaningless; he merely takes it for granted. He began by showing that they were ruled out by the verification principle; then he abandoned the verification principle because it ruled out moral statements, and adopted the use principle instead; finally he assumed that, while moral statements were now let in, metaphysical statements were still ruled out, but no demonstration was given of this. He has in fact been guilty of the same crime of unconscious 'cheating' as that of which Ayer was guilty in his mitigation of the verification principle, namely of stretching the rules sufficiently to let his favourites in, while still invoking them to keep his *bêtes noires* outside. He has also fallen into a glaring ambiguity in his use of the word 'empirical'. First of all, with impressive invocations of Locke, Hume, Mill and Russell, he used it to describe the position that all significant factual assertions must be about sensibly experienceable objects; then he used it to describe the position that all significant factual assertions must be such that it is possible to have a sensible experience of the way in which someone uses them. In this second sense, significance would have to be accorded to the most wildly metaphysical utterances of a Bradley or a Heidegger, for we can use our ears to hear what they say and our eyes to see what they write.

This, however, has been a digression, and we must return

to Braithwaite's main line of argument. What he is anxious to maintain is that religious statements have as their primary (though not their only) character their use as moral assertions; and it is for this reason, as he admits, that he has replaced the verification principle by the use principle. He thus goes on to inquire what interpretation of moral statements the use principle gives. He shows without difficulty that it is insufficient to say simply that moral statements are expressions of feeling of approval.

Discussion of the subject during the last twenty years has made it clear, I think, that no emotion or feeling of approval is fundamental to the use of moral assertions; it may be the case that the moral asserter has some specific feeling directed on to the course of action said to be right, but this is not the most important element in his 'pro-attitude' towards the course of action: what is primary is his intention to perform the action when the occasion for it arises.

The form of ethics without propositions which I shall adopt is therefore a conative rather than an emotive theory: it makes the primary use of a moral assertion that of expressing the intention of the asserter to act in a particular sort of way specified in the assertion.[1]

There is one peculiar advantage which Braithwaite claims for this view:

it alone enables a satisfactory answer to be given to the question: What is the reason for my doing what I think I ought to do? The answer it gives is that, since my thinking that I ought to do the action is my intention to do it if possible, the reason why I do the action is simply that I intend to do it, if possible. On every other ethical view there will be a mysterious gap to be filled somehow between the moral judgment and the intention to act in accordance with it: there is no such gap if the primary use of a moral assertion is to declare such an intention.[2]

[1] Ibid., p. 12.   [2] Op. cit., p. 14.

I find it very difficult to follow Braithwaite here. If it is true, as he holds, that my thinking that I ought to do the action *is* my intention to do it if possible, then it is not merely immoral for me to intend to do what I believe to be wrong but logically impossible. If it is true, as he says, that to declare that a course of action is right is to express one's intention to follow it if possible, then the man who says that he believes a certain act to be wrong but that he intends to do it all the same, is not merely an honest moral weakling or a hard-headed cynic; he is a muddle-headed thinker who does not know a contradiction in terms when he sees it. Now this seems to me to be contrary to all experience, and not to be at all the sort of position that an avowed empiricist should maintain. Surely one of the most obvious facts of moral experience is the sad fact that from time to time we not only do what is wrong—Braithwaite allows for that, when he says that a man 'will not necessarily be insincere in his assertion if he suspects, at the time of making it, that he will not have the strength of character to carry out his resolution'[1]—but only too often we *intend to do* what we *believe to be wrong*. If Braithwaite has never found himself in this position, he must be a very much better man than most of us.

Braithwaite's view of moral assertions thus seems to me to be quite impossible to maintain. This might, however, not be entirely fatal to his view of religious assertions, for he holds that religious assertions are something more than moral assertions, and even if he was wrong about the nature of moral assertions he might still be right about the way in which religious assertions were related to them. Now at first sight he might appear to be holding simply that a religious ssertion was one special kind of moral assertion.

[1] Ibid., p. 14.

> Just as the meaning of a moral assertion is given by its use in expressing the asserter's intention to act, so far as in him lies, in accordance with the moral principle involved, so the meaning of a religious assertion is given by its use in expressing the asserter's intention to follow a specified policy of behaviour.[1]

Braithwaite recognises, however, that, unlike moral assertions, religious assertions do not explicitly specify the policy which they involve. He replies, and I think the reply is a good one, that this does not matter, since the particular assertion is only one of the whole body of assertions which constitute the religious system in question: 'the body of assertions of which the particular one is a representative specimen is taken by the asserter as implicitly specifying a particular way of life'.[2] And he adds, once again claiming that in so doing he is loyal to the strictest principles of empiricism, that, when we make a scientific experiment, we are testing not one isolated hypothesis but the whole system of hypotheses of which it is a member.

Thus, for Braithwaite, 'the primary use of religious assertions is to announce allegiance to a set of moral principles: without such allegiance there is no "true religion"'.[3] He is not content to say, as Christian theologians have commonly said, that Christian behaviour is the normal consequence of Christian belief or the test of the extent to which it is something more than assent to a set of propositions; the behaviour *is* the belief, in the only valid sense that 'belief' can have. 'I myself,' he says, 'take the typical meaning of the body of Christian assertions as being given by their proclaiming intentions to follow an agapeistic way of life,'[4] and it is this and nothing more that he sees as being involved in the apparently factual assertion 'God is love.'[5] However, having

---

[1] Ibid., p. 15.   [2] Ibid., p. 17.   [3] Ibid., p. 19.   [4] Ibid.
[5] Ibid., p. 18.

E

made this startling identification of religious with moral assertions, he admits that there are certain differences between them.

> One is the fact already noticed that usually the behaviour policy intended is not specified by one religious assertion in isolation. Another difference is that the fundamental moral teaching of the religion is frequently given, not in abstract terms, but by means of concrete examples—of how to behave, for instance, if one meets a man set upon by thieves on the road to Jericho.[1]
>
> A more important difference . . . is that, in the higher religions at least, the conduct preached by the religion concerns not only external but also internal behaviour. . . . And though I have no doubt that the Christian concept of *agape* refers partly to external behaviour—the agapeistic behaviour for which there are external criteria—yet being filled with *agape* includes more than behaving agapeistically externally: it also includes an agapeistic frame of mind.[2]

However, Braithwaite admits that this cannot be all that is involved, since it can be plausibly maintained that religions which we cannot deny to be different religions may, at least in principle, recommend the same policy of life. 'How then can religious assertions be distinguished into those which are Christian, those which are Jewish, those which are Buddhist, by the policies of life which they respectively recommend if, on examination, these policies turn out to be the same?'[3]

One obvious answer is set aside at once, namely that the difference is simply a difference of ritual practices: 'There must be some more important difference between an agapeistically policied Christian and an agapeistically policied Jew than that the former attends a church and the latter a synagogue.'[4] I am myself inclined to think that this is the most important difference that there can be, but this is because I

---

[1] Ibid., p. 20.   [2] Ibid., p. 21.   [3] Ibid., p. 22.   [4] Ibid., p. 23.

believe that the Christian Eucharist is, in no 'Pickwickian' sense, the communication to men and women of the redemption which Christ won on Calvary, and their elevation into the life of God. But this, of course, is just the kind of thing that Braithwaite cannot say; it would go against all his empiricist principles. The really important difference for him is that in different religions the intentions to pursue the behaviour policies, which may or may not be the same, are associated with thinking of different stories. A 'story', we must notice, does not mean a set of metaphysical assertions; those, on Braithwaite's principles, would be nonsense. A story is 'a proposition or set of propositions which are straightforwardly empirical propositions capable of empirical test and which are thought of by the religious man in connexion with his resolution to follow the way of life advocated by his religion'.[1] The Christian thinks of one set of stories, and the Buddhist thinks of another. It is emphasised that, although the story is the sort of thing that might be true, since its propositions are all empirical, it is not asserted to be true by the believer; it is told or alluded to in the way in which one tells or alludes to the story of a novel which one has read.

3. COMMENTS AND CRITICISMS

The first comment which this astounding theory provokes is that, so far as Braithwaite's own empiricist principles are concerned, there seems to be no reason why the stories to which he refers should not only be entertained but should also be affirmed as true, since he himself says that all the propositions which they contain are empirical.[2] It looks as if this part of his theory derives not from his philosophical empiricism at all, but from a general reluctance to admit into the sphere of religious belief obligatory factual affirmations

[1] Ibid. [2] I am indebted for this point to Mr. T. H. McPherson.

of any kind. But, having said this, we must go on to remark
that he fails altogether to recognise how many different functions stories fulfil in Christian theology. There is first of all
the parable which was never intended to be factually true or
whose point is altogether unaffected by whether it is factually true or not. For example, the parable of the woman
searching the house for the lost coin in no way depends upon
whether Christ was referring to an actual incident; and in the
case of the parable of the husbandmen it is pretty clear that
he was not. Then there is the story which is deliberately
constructed by a theologian in order to bring out some aspect
of God's being or of his dealings with men; such, for example,
is the story of the Son proceeding from the Father like the
beam of light from a flame, or the story of the Atonement as
the paying of a fine in a criminal court on behalf of a bankrupt convict. Such stories are never adequate or exhaustive
expressions of the truth, and careful theologians are at pains
to point out at what point they fail to apply. On Braithwaite's own principles these stories would, I think, have to be
ruled out from the realm of factual assertions, for, however
sensory their language may be, theologians profess to use
them to describe realities that are not sensible. Whether
Braithwaite would include them among the Christian stories
which, although they cannot be believed, are to be entertained is not altogether clear. I shall argue later on that they
do make factual assertions, though they make them in a
peculiar way; this involves the rejection of Braithwaite's type
of empiricism, and we are not further concerned with them at
the moment. There is, however, a third type of story, namely
the stories of the life of Christ, which are related in the
Gospels: the story of his virginal conception, of his cruci-
fixion, of his rising from the dead, and so on. These
admittedly contain certain symbolical elements, when they deal

with certain non-sensible features of the events, as for example when in the stories of the temptation in the wilderness the devil is represented as having an oral conversation with Jesus and as locally transporting him to a pinnacle of the temple in Jerusalem. They also contain certain metaphysical assumptions of a type which Braithwaite's empiricism must reject as meaningless, as when they imply that Jesus possesses the authority of the Creator. But they also make a number of assertions about Jesus of a perfectly commonplace factual character: that he was born in Bethlehem, that he taught in Galilee, that he was crucified in Jerusalem by the orders of Pontius Pilate. Now Braithwaite makes no explicit reference to this last set of stories, but on his view they must be treated in exactly the same way as the rest; it is very important to think about them, but quite irrelevant whether any of them is true. One consequence of this is that it does not matter in the least to the Christian religion whether Jesus is an actual historical figure or merely a myth; we can think about the stories in either case. This complete irrelevance of factuality to Christianity is indeed recommended by Braithwaite as the strongest plank in his platform.

My contention that the propositional element in religious assertions consists of stories interpreted as straightforwardly empirical propositions which are not, generally speaking, believed to be true has the great advantage of imposing no restriction whatever upon the empirical interpretation which can be put upon the stories. The religious man may interpret the stories in the way which assists him best in carrying out the behaviour policies of his religion. . . . And since he need not believe the stories he can interpret them in ways which are not consistent with one another. . . . Indeed a story may provide better support for a long-range policy of action if it contains inconsistencies.[1]

[1] Op. cit., p. 29.

And he sums up his position as follows:

> A religious assertion, for me, is the assertion of an intention to
> carry out a certain behaviour policy, subsumable under a
> sufficiently general principle to be a moral one, together with
> the implicit or explicit statement, but not the assertion, of cer-
> tain stories.[1]

Thus there is in Braithwaite's system a double rejection of
factual statements. Statements which are avowedly theological, such as 'God exists,' 'God is love,' 'Jesus is God,'
and the like, are excluded as being non-empirical; but what
Braithwaite describes as 'the Christian stories' are excluded in
spite of being empirical, for some reason which is not stated
but which does not appear to be a philosophical reason at all.
They consist of statements which could indeed be meaningfully asserted, but which it is quite unimportant to assert,
though it is very important to entertain them. Whether
Braithwaite thinks that it would be harmful, as well as un-
necessary, to religion if the stories were not only entertained
but also asserted is not altogether clear. What does seem
clear, however, is that this part of his theory is logically un-
connected with his philosophical empiricism. There may,
however, be a psychological connection, for when once one
has rejected the great metaphysical and theological assertions
of the Christian Faith, no other assertions matter very much.

It may be added that on Braithwaite's principles there does
not seem to be any reason why a man should not belong to
several religions at once, for there is no reason why he should
not entertain a number of stories, if he is not obliged to
believe any of them, why he should not, for example, be a
Christian and a Buddhist as well. Many perfectly orthodox
Christians have entertained and been profoundly moved by

[1] Ibid., p. 32.

'the Christlike story of the king's son, who, having joy set before him, and protected from all pain and knowledge of suffering, yet abandoned all for compassion for the miseries of mankind'.[1] The reason why they do not become Buddhists is one that is irrelevant for Braithwaite, namely that they believe that Christian doctrine is true and that Buddhist doctrine is, in some important respects, false.

It is difficult, on reading Braithwaite's exposition of his position, not to feel that it manifests an extraordinary combination of sophistication and naïvety: of sophistication in that it is the kind of position that only a highly trained intellectual could devise, of naïvety in that it is difficult to see how any ordinary person (and the great bulk of those for whom Christianity is intended are ordinary persons) could think that Christianity was worth practising if he thought this position to be true. Braithwaite himself recognises that some people wonder what the function of the stories is if they need not be believed to be true. His answer is that great stories have a notably inspiring psychological effect upon people who read them. This, and the encouragement which people are able to give to one another, is the only substitute that he has to offer for that transformation of men and women by their elevation into the life of God which Christian theology knows by the name of supernatural grace.

It may sound like the typically bigoted sneer of a jaundiced cleric if one suggests that what Braithwaite is contending for is not Christianity at all, but I think that this would have been clear from his own exposition if he had been less evasive, in his discussion of the Christian 'stories', about those stories whose subject is Christ Himself. For, where St. Paul felt bound to write 'If Christ be not risen, then is your faith vain,' all that Braithwaite would be able to say is 'Even

[1] Victor White, God the Unknown, p. 94.

if Christ is not risen, you will find it an assistance in living an agapeistically policed life if you entertain, without necessarily believing them, the stories of the Resurrection appearances.' His final claim for the acceptance of his view is that 'whatever may be the case with other religions Christianity has always been a personal religion demanding personal commitment to a personal way of life'.[1] This is surely very much less than the truth. Whatever one may hold as to the necessity of accepting the Chalcedonian doctrine of the union of the two natures in the one divine Person of the eternal Son of God, it is surely undeniable that Christianity demands personal commitment not to a personal way of life (whatever that extremely vague phrase may mean), but to the concrete historical person Jesus of Nazareth. This, however, is just what Braithwaite's avowed principles will not allow him to say, whatever may be the implications of his religious practices. For to say this would be to imply that some at least of the Gospel stories were factually true, and indeed that the person of whom they tell is still alive and can be met with today. And this would be to assert the stories and not merely to entertain them.

Finally we must notice that Braithwaite fails altogether to explain in detail what is meant by living agapeistically and to give any reasons why a man should choose to live agapeistically rather than in some other way. He states the objection very fairly and fully, but his reply is remarkably weak.

We are all social animals; we are all members one of another. What is profitable to one man in helping him to persevere in the way of life he has decided upon may well be profitable to another man who is trying to follow a similar way of life; and to pass on information that might prove useful would be approved by almost every morality.[2]

[1] Op. cit., p. 34.   [2] Ibid., p. 33.

This, however, will be of no use in helping the man who has not yet decided what way of life to follow, and when he tries to answer this question Braithwaite becomes obscure in the extreme.

> All I will here say is that to hold that the adoption of a set of moral principles is a matter of the personal decision to live according to these principles does not imply that beliefs as to what are the practical consequences of following such principles are not relevant to the decision. An intention, it is true, cannot be logically based upon anything except another intention. But in considering what conduct to intend to practise, it is highly relevant whether or not the consequences of practising that conduct are such as one would intend to secure.[1]

But how, we now ask, are we to decide what consequences we intend to secure? Braithwaite has no way of telling us. And so it is in the last resort a matter of pure personal taste whether I am to be a Christian or a Buddhist or a Marxist.

There is a story of a Frenchman who went to a lecture on the Positivism of Auguste Comte. When the lecturer asked for questions, he rose with a puzzled expression and inquired whether he was really correct in supposing that the religion which had just been expounded was one in which it was not necessary to believe in the existence of God. The lecturer replied that he was quite right, and that this was the great advantage that this religion offered above all others. '*Religion sans Dieu?*' replied the questioner in amazement, '*Mon Dieu, quelle religion!*' And he sat down with a shrug of the shoulders. I cannot help feeling that Braithwaite's exposition might well provoke a similar reaction.

It must, I think, be admitted that Braithwaite does for the Christian religion just as much as it is possible to do for it if

[1] Ibid., p. 34.

one starts from a radically sensationalist position. All that it
leads us to is a form of Christianity without God, without
grace and, for all we can tell, without Christ, a religion in
which a policy of living for which no ground can be assigned
is bolstered up by the psychological encouragement that is
provided by entertaining, but not believing, the Christian
stories. If the starting point was inescapable, we should have
to be grateful for small mercies and make the best of a bad
job. Braithwaite nowhere shows, however, that no other
starting point is possible, and it is the chief purpose of the
present book to argue that there is a very different one which
is that of common sense and which is consistent with a much
more robust and satisfying faith. Professor Braithwaite at any
rate deserves our gratitude for the intrepidity with which he
has worked out the consequences of his initial assumption,
and for showing so clearly that if you start where he starts,
you are likely to end where he ends.[1]

[1] One is tempted to compare Professor Braithwaite's recasting of Christianity with the famous 'demythologising' programme of Dr. Rudolf Bultmann. Bultmann's rejection of the traditional interpretation of Christianity
on the ground that it postulates transcendental realities might seem to have
some affinity with the radical empiricism of Braithwaite; and Braithwaite's
entertaining of the Christian stories without necessarily believing them
might seem to be a less feverish Anglo-Saxon equivalent for Bultmann's
existentialist interpretation of Christian dogma and his Christianisation of
Heidegger. Furthermore, Braithwaite's failure to distinguish between the
different kinds of Christian stories provides a rough parallel to that inability
on the part of Bultmann to distinguish between different senses of 'myth' to
which Dr. A. M. Farrer has drawn attention in his concluding essay in the
English edition of *Kerygma and Myth*. However, the whole approach of the
New-Testament scholar Bultmann is so different from that of the philosopher
Braithwaite that I doubt whether it would be profitable to pursue the comparison further.

IV

TWO IDEALS OF KNOWLEDGE

1. INTELLECTUS *and* RATIO

IT is central to the position for which I am arguing that the intellect does not only reason, but also *apprehends*; it has, as its object, not only truths but *things*. This is what many modern philosophers overlook; for them all apprehension is done by the senses, the intellect only reasons. This point has been made very clearly by the German theologian Josef Pieper, as may be seen from the following extracts from his small book *Leisure the Basis of Culture*.

Is there such a thing [he asks] as a purely receptive attitude of mind in which we become aware of immaterial reality and invisible relationships? Is there such a thing as pure 'intellectual contemplation'—to adopt the terminology of the schools? In antiquity the answer given was always yes; in modern philosophy, for the most part, the answer given is no.

Kant, for example, held knowledge to be exclusively 'discursive': that is to say, the opposite of receptive and contemplative; and his opinion on this point has quite recently been called 'the most momentous dogmatic assumption of Kantian epistemology'. According to Kant man's knowledge is realised in the act of comparing, examining, relating, distinguishing, abstracting, deducing, demonstrating—all of which are forms of active intellectual effort. . . .

The philosophers of antiquity thought otherwise on this matter—though of course their view is very far from offering

63

grounds of justification for those who take the easy path. The Greeks—Aristotle no less than Plato—as well as the great medieval thinkers, held that not only physical, sensuous perception, but equally man's spiritual and intellectual knowledge, included an element of pure, receptive contemplation, or as Heraclitus says, of 'listening to the essence of things'.

'The Middle Ages,' he continues,

drew a distinction between the understanding as *ratio* and the understanding as *intellectus*. *Ratio* is the power of discursive, logical thought, of searching and of examination, of abstraction, of definition and drawing conclusions. *Intellectus*, on the other hand, is the name for the understanding in so far as it is the capacity of *simplex intuitus*, of that simple vision to which truth offers itself like a landscape to the eye. The faculty of mind, man's knowledge, is both these things in one, according to antiquity and the Middle Ages, simultaneously *ratio* and *intellectus*; and the process of knowing is the action of the two together. The mode of discursive thought is accompanied and impregnated by an effortless awareness, the contemplative vision of the *intellectus*, which is not active but passive, or rather receptive, the activity of the soul in which it conceives that which it sees.[1]

It needs to be added that this contemplative or receptive functioning of the mind as *intellectus* is not concerned simply with the apprehension of a purely spiritual or ideal realm; it is concerned equally with the perception of the everyday world of material things. The medievals at any rate were clear about this, even if the Greeks were not. The God whom Christians contemplate is the God whose creative activity is incessantly manifested in the existence of the finite world; he can be contemplated *in* his creatures, as well as apart from them. And in some respects the doctrine which I am supporting has more in common with the 'moderns' than with the Greeks, though

[1] Op. cit., pp. 31–4.

in other respects the opposite is true. It agrees with the moderns in holding that, in this life at any rate, all or almost all of our knowledge is mediated through the senses, but it agrees with the Greeks in holding that the mind has a contemplative as well as a ratiocinative function, that it is *intellectus* as well as *ratio*. It is the neglect of this twofold functioning of the human mind that has so drastically impoverished the mental life of the modern world and has produced the glacial and spectral character of much modern philosophy.

We can in fact set side by side two radically contrasted views of the ideal of human knowledge, and of the way in which the human mind should function if it is to achieve the full range of knowledge which is open to it. There is what we might conveniently call the 'modern' view, that in order to arrive at truth and avoid error the mind must, so far as is possible, detach itself from its object, attend only to the object's sensible characteristics, and confine its own activity to observation and ratiocination. There is, on the other hand, what I will call the 'traditional' view, which would hold that, while the 'modern' attitude is legitimate, and indeed necessary, for certain purposes, as for example the pursuit of the mathematical and physical sciences, the highest activity of the mind is one which requires not detachment from the object but involvement with it, not the restriction of attention to the sensible surface but penetration beneath it to the intelligible metaphysical being, not ratiocination but contemplation. The extension of the 'modern' attitude from its proper sphere to cover the whole range of cognitive activity can be traced back through the empiricists to Descartes, and it is the outcome of an excessive preoccupation with the problem of how to avoid error.

The very foundation of the Cartesian philosophy was the search for some absolutely certain and indisputable truth or truths, upon which the whole structure of knowledge could be subsequently erected, some pellucidly clear and distinct idea which would carry its own authentication. Such truths Descartes believed he had discovered in the affirmation of his own existence and of the existence of God, the former being based upon the famous *cogito ergo sum* and the latter upon the ontological argument; and on the basis of these two truths he proceeded to argue, as is well known, for the existence of an external world as a real counterpart of the world of ideas which he found in his own mind. It was easy for Descartes' critics to point out that the most which the *cogito* could prove was the existence of a momentary subject of a momentary experience; and when in addition the shakiness of the ontological argument had been made manifest, both the mind as a persisting substance and the external world as a real existent vanished and all that remained of Descartes' system was the ideas. There is thus a direct transition, *via* Locke and Berkeley, from the radical idealism of Descartes to the radical sensationalism of Hume, for whom sense-impressions were the only real existents, and both minds and physical objects were merely bundles of sense-impressions. It is instructive to recall that when, in the present century, the sensationalist empiricism of Hume was revived in the doctrine that the immediate objects of our awareness are sense-data and that physical objects are logical constructs from these, it was with the deliberate intention of taking as the basic entities of the world objects about whose nature we could not possibly be deceived; what I had taken to be a black cat on the chair might turn out to be a lady's muff, but at least I was not wrong in seeing a black furry patch.[1] A very similar position was

[1] The vicissitudes of the sense-datum discussion may be followed in such works as G. E. Moore, *Philosophical Studies*, ch. v; B. Russell, *Our Knowledge of the External World*, ch. iii; H. H. Price, *Perception*.

that of Wittgenstein and the logical atomists, although for them the fundamental constituents of the universe were not objects but facts. In Professor J. O. Urmson's words, 'if we call Hume's doctrine that the objects of human experience, the ultimate particulars, are impressions his metaphysical thesis, we see that the metaphysics of logical atomism in Wittgenstein's version differed from it mainly in the substitution of sensibly given facts for sensibly given particulars as the ultimate data'.[1] However, as Professor Urmson has shown in the book from which I have just quoted, neither form of sensationalism was able to maintain its position; for it became clear that if you formed any judgment about the alleged ultimate or even described its sensible character you were raising the question of its relation to other constituents of the world and so were not proof against the possibility of error. The retreat from an external world into a world of sense-data having failed to provide a basis of infallible knowledge, the next move in the search for certainty was a further retreat from the world of sense-data into the world of language; so that the whole problem of the relation of perception to reality was by-passed as insoluble or unintelligible, and philosophy became a branch of philology or even of anthropology, the study of the linguistic habits of philosophers, scientists and ordinary men. Further than this the attitude of detachment could hardly go, and there are welcome signs in more than one quarter of a reaction towards a more metaphysical view of philosophy.

In passing, it may be well to warn the unwary reader not to be deluded by the fact that many philosophers whose position is fundamentally sensationalist or linguistic are found on occasion giving somewhat anxious assurances of their belief

[1] *Philosophical Analysis: its Development between the two World Wars*, p. 108.

in the existence of physical objects, their own minds and people other than themselves. Philosophers are in fact generally concerned to persuade the ordinary man that they are not taking away from him anything in which he believes; just so, we may remember, Berkeley in the person of Philonous maintained that his theory of sensible things was really the commonsense view. 'I am content, Hylas,' he wrote,

> to appeal to the common sense of the world for the truth of my notion. Ask the gardener, why he thinks yonder cherry-tree exists in the garden, and he shall tell you, because he sees and feels it; in a word, because he perceives it by his senses. Ask him, why he thinks an orange tree not to be there, and he shall tell you, because he does not perceive it. What he perceives by sense, that he terms a real being, and saith it *is* or *exists*; but that which is not perceivable, the same, he saith, hath no being.[1]

In a very similar vein, Ayer wrote as follows:

> It is common for writers on the subject of perception to assume that, unless one can give a satisfactory analysis of perceptual situations, one is not entitled to believe in the existence of material things. But this is a complete mistake. What gives one the right to believe in the existence of a certain material thing is simply the fact that one has certain sensations: for, whether one realises it or not, to say that the thing exists is equivalent to saying that such sensations are obtainable. It is the philosopher's business to give a correct definition of material things in terms of sensations. But his success or failure in this task has no bearing whatsoever on the validity of our perceptual judgments. That depends wholly on actual sense-experience.[2]

An incautious reader might well suppose that in this passage Ayer was expressing a wholehearted physical realism, that he

---

[1] *Dialogues*, III (Everyman edition, p. 270).
[2] *Language, Truth and Logic*, 2nd ed., p. 50.

was telling us that, whether the philosophers can explain it or not, our senses reveal to us that there is a world of physical objects which are either material substances or at the least are permanent complexes of physical qualities. Such a supposition would be totally false. For the whole context of the passage shows that the 'existence' which is predicated of material things is merely the occurrence of their names in the language by means of which we describe our sense-experience. It means nothing more than the assertion that rules can be given by the use of which, from sentences containing words like 'chair', and 'dog', we can be led to formulate other sentences the nouns in which are simply the names of sensible particulars.[1]

The situation is very much the same as regards Professor Gilbert Ryle's use of the word 'mind'. He is extremely anxious not to eliminate from our vocabulary either this word or the adjectives which have usually been held to describe mental states and dispositions, such as 'cautious', 'intrepid'. 'sagacious', 'obstinate', 'weary' and the like. But it is of the very heart of his position to deny that there are substances called minds, to whose qualities these adjectives refer; to hold otherwise would, for him, be to fall into the error which, with what he himself calls 'deliberate abusiveness', he derides as the Cartesian 'dogma of the Ghost in the Machine'.[2] For him, the words which are commonly taken to denote mental processes or characteristics do nothing more than describe the way in which certain sensibly observable processes occur, or certain of their sensibly observable characteristics. 'To

[1] Cf. Ayer, *Foundations of Empirical Knowledge*, p. 156: 'The facts we express by referring to sense-data are, for the most part, the same as those that we ordinarily express by referring to material things. And all that is meant by speaking of "construction" or "analysis" in this case is that one terminology is to be exhibited as a function of the other.'

[2] *The Concept of Mind*, p. 15.

F

find that most people have minds,' he writes, 'is *simply* to find that they are able and prone to do certain sorts of things, and this we do by witnessing the sorts of things they do.'[1] And again: 'Overt intelligent performances are not clues to the workings of minds; they *are* those workings.'[2] It is clear that for Ryle, the relation of the mind to the body is in essentials the same as is (or was[3]) the relation of physical objects to sensible particulars for Ayer. Neither the mind in the one case nor the physical object in the other has reality in the old-fashioned metaphysical sense, but it would be denied that either of them was being accused of non-reality. On the contrary, it would be asserted that to each of them was being accorded the only kind of reality that by its nature it could have; namely, reality as a word in a language-system in which, by the application of agreed conventions of interpretation, sentences containing mental words or physical-object words can be translated into sentences about bodily behaviour or sensible particulars respectively.

2. THINGS, PERSONS AND GOD

The fundamental assertions of my position are these. First, that, although perception normally takes place through the medium of sensation, its essence is not sense-awareness but intellectual apprehension; the intellect uses the sensible phenomenon as an *objectum quo*, through which its passes to the apprehension of the *objectum quod* which is the intelligible trans-sensible being. Hence, in the second place, the intelligible object is not something whose existence is *deduced from* that of the sensible phenomena, as Locke thought, nor is it

[1] Ibid., p. 61 (italics mine).

[2] Ibid., p. 58 (italics mine).

[3] For some of Ayer's later writings show signs of a retreat to a more traditional position, e.g. his recent book *The Problem of Knowledge*.

something mentally *constructed out of* the sensible phenomena, as many modern empiricists have held, but something *grasped through* them. Thirdly, in order to penetrate beneath the sensible phenomena to the real intelligible things that support them, we need, not an attitude of detachment, ratiocination and attention to the phenomenal surface of things, useful as this is for certain purposes, but an attitude of involvement, contemplation and penetration into their intelligible depths. Only so, I believe, is it possible for us to apprehend that unique but universal characteristic of finite beings which manifests their dependence upon the creative activity of a transcendent cause, the God of Christian theology.

It is not, however, Christian theology alone that is at stake here, but any belief in the existence of real objects outside our minds, both physical objects and other persons as well as God. The insoluble problem of the sensationalist philosopher is that of getting to the far side of his own sensations, to the world of cats and cabbages and human beings. For since, on his own principles, all the material of his knowledge consists of his own sensations, his experience will be exactly the same whether there is a trans-sensible world or not, provided only that the sensations occur. Descartes at any rate was conscious of the difficulty, and he found it necessary to appeal to the truthfulness of God for a guarantee that anything existed except his own mind. More modern philosophers, rightly recognising that God cannot be brought in in just this way, have failed to solve the problem at all. Lord Russell, for example, in some of his earlier works admitted frankly his inability to produce arguments against the solipsist position, though he had no hesitation in rejecting it. 'In actual fact,' he wrote, 'whatever we may try to think as philosophers, we cannot help believing in the minds of other people, so that the question whether our belief is justified has a merely speculative interest'[1]—a somewhat surprising statement from a philosopher whose profession was speculation. Elsewhere he remarked that solipsism is 'hard to refute, but still harder to believe', and told an amusing story about a letter which he had received from a philosopher who was a solipsist and who expressed surprise that solipsists were not more common. His comment, 'This shows that solipsism is not really believed even by those who think they are convinced of its truth,'[2] while perfectly just, does nothing to meet the simple objection that solipsism cannot be disproved on sensationalist principles. Professor Ryle, in his famous work *The Concept of Mind*, has no difficulty in showing that, in the meaning which he gives to 'mind', there is just as much reason for me to assert that other people have minds as to assert that I myself have a mind; this is, however, cold comfort since he does not believe that either I myself or anybody else has a mind in the ordinary sense of the term. For him mental terms simply denote characteristics of overt bodily behaviour, and he even goes so far as to say that there is no essential difference between knowing ourselves and knowing other people.

I learn that a certain pupil of mine is lazy, ambitious and witty by following his work, noticing his excuses, listening to his conversation and comparing his performances with those of others. Nor does it make any important difference if I happen myself to be that pupil. I can then indeed listen to more of his conversations, as I am the addressee of his unspoken soliloquies; I notice more of his excuses, as I am never absent, when they are made. On the other hand, my comparison of his performances with those of others is more difficult, since the examiner is himself taking the examination. . . .[3]

---

[1] *Our Knowledge of the External World*, 2nd ed., p. 104.
[2] *Outline of Philosophy*, p. 302. Cf. *Human Knowledge: its Scope and Limits*, p. 196.   [3] Op. cit., p. 169.

It is clear that Ryle manages to retain a belief in the existence of the minds of other people only by redefining the term 'mind' in a way which reduces both their minds and his to a merely adverbial status as modes of bodily behaviour; this is not surprising, since the particular type of behaviourism which he affects is as extreme an example as could be found of the theory which I am attacking, the theory which sets up the ideals of detachment, ratiocination and attention to phenomena.

It is, of course, possible for the consistent phenomenalist to say that it does not matter whether other minds than his own exist or not, since in any case all he can perceive will be the sensible phenomena. Indeed he may well dismiss the distinction as meaningless. (On the basis of his verification principle one would expect Professor Ayer to do this, though in fact with remarkable inconsistency he refuses to do so.[1]) Even if it is significant to assert that there is a real sentient being behind the sensible phenomena which are commonly described as his wife, the phenomenalist must affirm that it is a matter of complete unimportance whether the assertion is true or false, since all he can perceive are the phenomena and they will be the same in either case. The position needs only to be stated in this way for its falsity to be apparent. What a man is in love with is not a set of sensible phenomena but a living sentient being which he believes to be in many ways like, and perhaps in more ways unlike, himself. He will not be satisfied if he is offered in exchange a set of depthless and hollow phenomena, even if he is assured that he will not be able to tell the difference. He will not in fact admit that all

---

[1] *Foundations of Empirical Knowledge*, ch. iii, 'The Egocentric Predicament'. Cf. *Philosophical Essays*, ch. viii, 'One's Knowledge of Other Minds'. It is notable that in neither of these discussions is the verification principle mentioned.

that he perceives are the phenomena; he will tell you that the phenomena are media through which he grasps, however obscurely, an intelligible and intelligent being. Nor will he be shaken in this assertion if you point out that he is sometimes unable to tell the difference between the real wife and what even he must admit to be a mere set of sensible phenomena, as on the occasion when he lifted his hat in greeting to the reflection of his wife in a mirror. He will merely answer that he is not infallible and that it is possible to misuse your *objecta quibus* as well as to use them; that in employing sensible phenomena as its instruments his intellect sometimes makes mistakes. The point is well brought out in Charles Williams's novel *Descent into Hell*, though I doubt whether its author thought of applying it to our present concern. In that story a man is in love with a girl who fails to respond to his passion. By the sheer force of his desire, though without any conscious effort to do so or indeed any suspicion of its possibility, he finds he has brought into being a phantom replica of the girl which has every physical property and disposition of the girl herself and is, so far as the sensible phenomena are concerned, altogether indistinguishable from her. On phenomenalist and behaviourist principles the phantom ought to have done just as well as the real woman, for as regards the sensory experiences to be derived from them the two were simply identical. The moral of the story is, however, that so far from the phantom doing just as well it led the man to madness and ultimately to hell. Like the damned in Dante's *Commedia*, he had lost the good of the intellect.

It may perhaps appear as if the argument which I have put forward amounts to little more than a plea for woolly thinking. That is emphatically not so. But I do deny the Cartesian thesis that knowledge cannot be knowledge at all unless it is clear and distinct, the thesis which, in spite of his

violent repudiation of Cartesianism, is the dominant characteristic of the philosophy of Professor Ryle. The inevitable
consequence of the view that knowledge must be clear and
distinct is that if there is any sphere of reality that by its
nature cannot be known clearly and distinctly it cannot be
known at all. Physical objects, other persons, and God will
alike be eliminated, or at best will be redefined in terms of
phenomena, in order to conform with the criterion that has
been adopted. When mind has been reduced to the overt
dispositional characters of human bodily behaviour it is not
really surprising that Professor Ryle should commit himself
to the otherwise astounding assertion that people 'are relatively tractable and relatively easy to understand',[1] he has got
rid of everything in them that is not. Nor is it surprising that
the world of the linguistic empiricists has an extraordinarily
glacial, emaciated and sterile character. It is a world in which
depth has been sacrificed to clarity, and in which nothing has
any inside, a world in which there are no questions left to
answer, not because they have all been answered but because
they have been condemned as being no questions at all.
'Philosophy,' wrote Ludwig Wittgenstein in his later years,
in words which are a far cry from the 'mysticism' of the
Tractatus Logico-Philosophicus, 'simply puts everything
before us, and neither explains nor deduces anything. Since
everything lies open to view there is nothing to explain.'[2]
Such a conclusion is the inevitable outcome of the Cartesian
obsession with clarity and distinctness; it excludes from its
scope the major part of the world of our experience. Like a
diet consisting entirely of disinfectants, it may preserve you
from poisoning, but only at the expense of starvation. It is
possible to carry the maxim 'Safety first' too far.

My contention then is that we have a whole range of

[1] Op. cit., p. 114.   [2] *Philosophical Investigations*, I, 126.

knowledge, knowledge not *of* but *through* sensible phenomena, which is essentially obscure and opaque; it includes in its scope some of the most important aspects of our experience, such as our knowledge of physical objects, other persons and God. This involves a complete repudiation of Descartes' view that we can have a clear and distinct idea of God by the exercise of our natural powers; whatever may be true about the supernatural condition of the beatific vision, here we know God through a glass darkly and not face to face. Nevertheless, our knowledge of God, like our knowledge of physical objects and other persons, while obscure and opaque is genuine knowledge. It is partial, inchoate and subject to error, but it is not incurably fallacious; for the mind, though fallible, is self-correcting. It can make mistakes, but it can also discover that it has made them and can put them right; this may be surprising but it is the fact.

Thus, over against the Cartesian view of the world as an exhaustively intelligible presentation lying patiently before us for our detached and dispassionate examination—a world which, as it were, has all the goods in the shop window and nothing beneath the counter—we must set the view of the world as essentially mysterious and yet not entirely alien to us, a world into which we can penetrate in part and which we can know in part, but only if we approach it in the attitude of contemplation and humility. I believe indeed that the notion of mystery is essential to the position which I am defending, and I shall therefore devote a little space to its consideration.

3. Puzzles, Problems and Mysteries

I shall begin by distinguishing between what I shall call, I hope with not too much violence to common usage, puzzles, problems and mysteries.[1] By a *puzzle* I mean something which purports to be a genuine question requiring an answer, but turns out upon investigation to be merely a pseudo-question which vanishes into thin air when the terms in which it is stated are examined. Such, for example, would be the perplexing assertion that a monosyllable eats fish, based upon the undeniable premises that (i) a cat eats fish, and (ii) cat is a monosyllable. Once this argument has been shown to rest upon a confusion between formal and material supposition (that is, roughly, between the use of a word to stand for a thing and the use of it to stand for itself) nothing more remains to be investigated. The question 'How can a monosyllable eat anything?', which was formerly in the mind, ceases to need an answer, since the argument which purported to prove that a monosyllable could eat something has been shown to be fallacious. If the anti-metaphysical linguistic analysts are right, all metaphysical questions are puzzles in this sense. It is for Ayer simply a matter of logic that, for example, each person's experience is private to himself.[2] On similar grounds, Ryle and Ayer have dismissed the so-called 'problem of the relation between soul and body'.[3]

By a problem I mean a question which does not evaporate on linguistic analysis and which we cease to ask only when we have discovered the answer. Most of the questions of science and mathematics are of this kind and so are many of the questions which arise in daily life. 'Can a single-valued analytic function have three periods?', 'How many electrons are there in the outer ring of the dysprosium atom?', 'What

[1] The distinction between these three terms is made by Dr. A. M. Farrer in *The Glass of Vision*, ch. iv and v, but his meanings, while they are similar to mine, are not entirely identical with them. He derives the distinction between problems and mysteries from M. Gabriel Marcel.

[2] Cf. *Foundations of Empirical Knowledge*, ch. iii.

[3] Cf. *The Physical Basis of Mind*, ed. P. Laslett, p. 70 f.

is the best way to get rid of a cold in the head?', 'What did Richard III have to eat before the Battle of Bosworth?' These are questions of very different kinds, and their answers must be sought in different ways. Some of them need empirical investigation, while some require the exercise of pure thought. But they are all alike in the fact that they are satisfied only by being answered. It should be noticed that the so-called 'mystery stories' which are so popular an element in modern literature are mostly concerned with problems and not with mysteries in the sense in which I am about to define that word. Nor are they, at any rate normally, puzzles. 'Who killed Charlie Winpole?' is, for example, the title of a story by the late Ernest Bramah, and the reader's curiosity is satisfied when he is told who killed Charlie Winpole; he does not expect the author to demonstrate that he had really been stating only a pseudo-question. It is not of course always easy to know whether a particular form of words is expressing a puzzle or a problem; thus 'Why is the rate of change of momentum of a massive body proportional to the impressed force?' will be a puzzle if we believe, with some philosophers of science, that Newton's second law of motion is a definition of force, but it will be a problem if we believe with others that it is an empirical generalisation. Nevertheless, the distinction between puzzles and problems is a clear one, and they are both of them very different from what I shall describe as a *mystery*.

In the first place, although the contemplation of a mystery may raise questions which we desire to answer, a mystery is not in itself a question demanding an answer, but an object inviting contemplation. It shares with a problem the character of being something of which we are to a greater or less degree ignorant and with which we wish to become better acquainted; but the activity to which it invites us is not that of standing back and viewing it in detachment as something subject to our condescending investigation, but that of penetrating beneath its surface in an attitude of humble and wondering contemplation. There are in fact three features which belong to a mystery, as I am now using the term. In the first place, on being confronted with a mystery we are conscious that the small central area of which we have a relatively clear vision shades off into a vast background which is obscure and as yet unpenetrated. Secondly, we find, as we attempt to penetrate this background in what I have described as an attitude of humble and wondering contemplation, that the range and clarity of our vision progressively increase but that at the same time the background which is obscure and unpenetrated is seen to be far greater than we had recognised before. It is in fact rather as if we were walking into a fog with the aid of a lamp which was steadily getting brighter; the area which we could see with some distinctness would get larger and larger but so also would the opaque and undifferentiated background in which no detail was yet visible. Thus, in the contemplation of a mystery there go together in a remarkable way an increase both of knowledge and also of what we might call conscious ignorance. The third feature of a mystery to which I want to draw attention is the fact that a mystery, while it remains obscure in itself, has a remarkable capacity of illuminating other things.

It would be easiest to demonstrate this threefold character of mysteries and their contemplation by reference to the great revealed mysteries of the Christian Faith, for example the Trinity and the Incarnation. We should see how the gradual formulation of the Church's dogmas in more and more precise terms went hand in hand with a growing understanding of the necessarily analogical character of the terms and concepts employed and of the essentially unique and transcendent nature of the truths and realities under consideration. We should also see how the Church's understanding of matters that were not in the narrow sense religious had been deepened as a result of the light shed upon them by the Christian mysteries; how, for example, the notion of the human being, as a responsible person, with a dignity that cannot be destroyed and a value for all eternity, had been enhanced by the doctrines of the tri-personality of God and of the assumption of human nature by God in the Incarnation. Here, however, we are concerned with natural and not with supernatural mysteries, and my point is that, in order to penetrate the phenomenal skin of the perceptual world in order to grasp either physical objects or human persons or the God who is the creator and sustainer of both, we must learn to contemplate them with humility and wonder and not merely to record their sensible qualities and analyse their relationships. The element of wonder is of the highest importance here, and we must note that the wonder which is associated with contemplation does not consist of wondering what the answer to certain questions may be— for example, wondering how many electrons there are in the outer ring of the dysprosium atom—but simply of wondering *at* finite beings themselves. It is the wonder which led the entomologist in Charles Williams's novel *The Place of the Lion*, when he had seen all the butterflies in the world, with all their several and distinctive beauties, coalesced into one supreme and archetypal insect, to wander about open-mouthed repeating the words 'Glory, glory!' Or is it the wonder of the child at the stupendously surprising character of the world in which he finds himself, the wonder which that profoundly childlike man Gilbert Chesterton kept throughout his life and which he expressed in his poem 'A Second Childhood.'

When all my days are ending
   And I have no song to sing,
I think I shall not be too old
   To stare at everything;
As I stared once at a nursery door
   Or a tall tree and a swing. . . .

Men grow too old for love, my love,
   Men grow too old for lies;
But I shall not grow too old to see
   Enormous night arise,
A cloud that is larger than the world
   And a monster made of eyes. . . .

Men grow too old to woo, my love,
   Men grow too old to wed:
But I shall not grow too old to see
   Hung crazily overhead
Incredible rafters when I wake
   And find I am not dead. . . .

Strange crawling carpets of the grass,
   Wide windows of the sky:
So in this perilous grace of God
   With all my sins go I:
And things grow new though I grow old,
   Though I grow old and die.

Briefly, this attitude of wonder which goes with contemplation is not wondering *how* or wondering *whether*, legitimate as those activities are in their place, it is wondering *at*. It is fundamentally connected with the principle which I have repeatedly asserted, namely that our perception of the world need not and, unless it is deliberately inhibited, will not terminate in the sensible phenomenon. It is, of course, possible

for us, by a kind of self-denying ordinance, to arrest perception at the level of the phenomenon, though I doubt whether
it is psychologically possible for anyone to do so for long.
And if we do so arrest it we shall be simply confronted with
an extended continuum which has no depth and poses no
questions. Our perceptions will approximate to what Whitehead described as 'perception in the mode of presentational
immediacy'. Normally, however, perception does not so terminate; the mind penetrates beneath the phenomenon and
acquires an obscure but none the less genuine grasp of an intelligible trans-sensible being. Using a different metaphor,
we might say that the mind uses the phenomenon as a step-
ping stone to higher things, for in these matters, as in mystical theology, the images of height and depth seem equally
appropriate. In Thomist language, the intellect abstracts the
intelligible essence from the sensible species and is united to
it in the concept. In Whitehead's jargon, perception in the
mode of presentational immediacy is supplemented by perception in the mode of causal efficacy. I do not think it
matters very much how we express the fact at issue, though I
should be reluctant to endorse Whitehead's doctrine of the
'symbolic reference' which he sees as relating the two
modes.[1] (I should, however, like to remark upon the insight
with which, in spite of his warm sympathy for John Locke,
he sees Locke's radical defect as lying in the adoption of a
representative doctrine of perception.) My concern at the
moment is to emphasise the essentially obscure nature of our
apprehension of trans-sensible entities in the act of contemplative penetration. This applies equally whether we penetrate simply as far as the physical object, or to the human
person whose body the physical object may be, or to the God
whose creative efficacy is at the root of physical objects and

[1] *Process and Reality*, Part II, ch. viii. Cf. *Symbolism*, passim.

human persons alike. In each case the object is a *mystery*, in the sense in which I have used the word, and our grasp of it is correspondingly obscure. It will, however, partake of the three characteristics which I have previously ascribed to our knowledge of mysteries. As we penetrate into it both our knowledge of it and our recognition of the extent to which it transcends our knowledge will increase, and although our knowledge of it will remain obscure and partial it will bring with it an increasing understanding of other things.

It is because God is a mystery in this sense that to anyone who is a practising theist Professor Flew's elimination of theism is bound to appear somewhat lacking in inside knowledge. For the Christian does not simply give intellectual assent to the proposition 'God is love' and then, when confronted with hostile evidence, glibly redefine his terms so that the proposition will still be true. He gets to know God better and better the longer he lives in the world, and comes more and more to know as a matter of personal experience how very much more profound and paradoxical a thing the love of God is than he had previously realised.

The way in which this happens is too elaborate to be briefly described; and it partakes of the character of mystery which belongs to its object. It will certainly not derive simply from the contemplation of the natural world, and if the man in question is a Christian it will be mediated to him largely through the life of the Church and participation in the sacraments. Nevertheless, the contemplation of the natural world will play its part in this; and, since, as Professor H. J. Paton has pointed out in his Gifford Lectures,[1] the very possibility of such an approach to God has been called in question in recent years in both philosophical and theological quarters, I

[1] *The Modern Predicament*, ch. ii, iii.

shall conclude this chapter with some short remarks on the possibility of natural theology.

Natural theology is the passage from the recognition of the existence of the finite world to the affirmation of the existence of God. Its legitimacy therefore depends upon whether this passage can be validly made; and the case of the anti-metaphysicians is that it clearly cannot. Nothing whatever is implied by the existence of one particular about the existence of another. Furthermore, all our language is defined in terms of sense-objects, and nobody claims to define God in terms of sense-objects; therefore, nothing can be significantly said about God, not even that he exists.

Now it must be admitted that these objections have considerable force against natural theology as it has been, and indeed still is, understood in certain quarters. It has, for example, been maintained by some scholastics that the famous 'Five Ways' by which St. Thomas Aquinas argues for the existence of God are pure exercises in syllogistic deduction; that the premises 'If anything exists, God exists' and 'Something does exist' logically imply the conclusion 'Therefore God exists' by the simple application of the mood *ponendo ponems* of the hypothetical syllogism. Their difficulty is how to prove the truth of the major premise without already begging the conclusion, and I for one cannot see how this can be done. There is, however, another school of thought, of which, in spite of their differences on points of detail, Dr. A. M. Farrer, Dom Mark Pontifex and Dom Illtyd Trethowan are representative, according to which the function of the arguments is to direct the attention of the mind to certain features of finite beings which can easily be overlooked and from which the existence of God can be seen without a discursive process. There is no question of asserting that, in this movement, we have a direct and immediate apprehension of God; direct, if you like, but not immediate, for it is mediated by and in our apprehension of finite beings. For Pontifex and Trethowan,[1] if we grasp the existence of finite beings as it truly is we shall see that it is simply identical with their relation to the transcendent cause which is their Creator; for Farrer, we shall similarly grasp what he calls the 'cosmological idea', the idea of God-and-the-creature-in-relation.[2] It is not denied that in making this approach there is a great deal to be done in the way of argument and discussion; but it would be held that the purpose of this argument and discussion is not to win assent to a logical demonstration, but to put the hearer in the frame of mind in which he will be able to apprehend finite beings as they really are, to get beyond both the superficial level of sensible phenomena and also beyond even the particular individual existence of the finite beings themselves, to the Creator upon whose incessant activity their very existence depends. What can thus be apprehended, it is alleged, is neither the-creature-without-God nor God-without-the-creature, but the-creature-deriving-being-from-God and God-as-the-creative-ground-of-the-creature: God-and-the-creature-in-the-cosmological-relation. To use another term, there is a *contuition* of God, 'the apprehension of the presence of the cause in a perceived effect'.[3]

I have expounded this view of the nature of natural theology in considerable detail elsewhere[4] and there is no need for detailed repetition here. It will, however, be well to point out that the power of contuition, to which I have just referred, needs training like any other skill. It will not come easily to anyone who has never learnt the art of contemplative reflec-

---

[1] *The Meaning of Existence*, passim.   [2] *Finite and Infinite*, part I.
[3] Cf. *Mediaeval Mystical Tradition and Saint John of the Cross*, by a Benedictine of Stanbrook, p. 70.
[4] *He Who Is*, ch. vi, vii; *Existence and Analogy*, ch. iv.

G

tion or, on the other hand, to anyone who has been trained into the condition of perceptual myopia in which awareness of the external world is arrested at the level of the sensible phenomena and in which the intellect functions almost exclusively as *ratio*, in the discursive mode. If, however, the power of contuition needs training, this does not mean that it is u.mnatural or artificial; the power of walking needs training, and it is not unnatural or artificial either. There is in fact a good deal of reason for supposing that in less sophisticated societies than ours the contemplative contuition of God in nature is a perfectly normal human activity. There are of course two ways of explaining the fact that we have very largely lost this skill, and it is not easy on general grounds to decide between them. It can be asserted that the human race, in its more civilised sections, has at last cast off the age-long shackles of superstition and has entered upon its rightful heritage in a godless universe. Or it can equally well be asserted that the conditions of life in our modern industrialised societies have largely atrophied a normal human faculty. There are, I believe, substantial grounds for accepting the second of these interpretations, but they are not our precise concern at the moment. Clearly our apprehension of God as the creative ground of physical objects will be more obscure than our apprehension of physical objects as the ontological ground of sensible phenomena; God lies one stage farther back than they, and he transcends our finite understanding as no finite being transcends it. We need not be surprised, therefore, if there are many people, even in our modern world, who find no difficulty in apprehending the existence of their wives or their cats but considerable difficulty in apprehending the existence of God. Human finitude is sufficient to account for this, even if we leave out of consideration the peculiar dimming of our intellect in its higher spheres of operation which Christian theology holds to be one of the fruits of human sin. Even under the most favourable conditions our perception of God is bound to be exceedingly partial and obscure; Christian theology maintains that this, among other reasons, is why God has supplemented our natural knowledge of him by a supernatural revelation.

It will be obvious that we are at this point upon the brink of an exposition of the whole subject of natural theology; I must resist the temptation to cross that brink. The purpose of this chapter has been more modest. It has been to argue that, side by side with the detached, critical and discursive function of the human mind there is another which is no less necessary and natural, which is marked by involvement, sympathy and contemplation. The knowledge which we achieve in this second way is of necessity partial and obscure; like its objects it partakes of the nature of mystery. But many of the most important realms of reality can be reached only in this way; they include physical objects, persons other than ourselves and, supremely, the transcendent and creative God. If we set up the first type of mental activity as the exclusive ideal, we may perhaps avoid error, though even that is doubtful, but we shall certainly avoid everything else. It is through the second type of activity that we reach the things that really matter.

V

KNOWLEDGE AND COMMUNICATION

1. SPEECH AND THOUGHT

WHETHER we can know an object is not precisely the same question as whether we can talk about it, true though it is that, at any rate normally, we can communicate our thoughts only by the use of written or spoken words. Indeed, even our private thinking is vastly assisted by the activity which we describe as 'talking to ourselves', although a certain school of behaviourists exaggerates disgracefully when it asserts that thinking is nothing more than a kind of rudimentary or subliminal talk, an imperceptible muscular exercise of our larynxes. Certainly our power to communicate to others the thoughts that are in our own minds and to receive into our minds the thoughts that are in theirs depends quite indispensably upon our power to emit and to apprehend spoken or written words; and this is as true of our thoughts about God as of our thoughts about anything else. I wish, therefore, in the present chapter to discuss the relation of words to thought and communication, and in particular to the communication of our ideas about God and of our experience of his dealings with us.

There is a commonly held view according to which our power to communicate our thoughts to other people is conceived simply in terms of communication-engineering. We code our thoughts into words, and the other party to the conversation decodes them into thoughts again; and the accuracy of the reproduction depends simply upon the extent to which both the coding and the decoding processes approximate to processes with a one-one correlation, an approximation which can never be complete. If, for example, I am a newspaper correspondent telegraphing to my paper an account of the Boat Race, I can never hope to reproduce in my message all the features of my impression of the event, though I can hope with luck to reproduce those that my employers consider to be most important, such as the name of the winning crew and the distance by which it won. It will be instructive to see how theological discourse between two persons will be envisaged if the model of coding and decoding a message is taken as expressing the whole truth.

We have to suppose to begin with that the two parties to the conversation are fortunate in the possession of a common language, English for example, by means of which they are able to label with the same names sensible objects which are roughly similar. There may, of course, be a certain penumbra of vagueness about this; one of them may apply the name 'tree' to two objects indifferently, while the other will distinguish them as respectively an 'oak' and an 'elm'. Still, neither of them will apply the name 'tree' to the object to which the other will apply the name 'tin-opener', and so long as they are talking about ordinary objects of everyday life they will get along quite happily with only occasional misunderstandings. How this more or less common vocabulary was acquired in the first place may indeed be somewhat mysterious, but we do in fact manage to acquire its elements in childhood, by a process in which ostensive definition by our elders plays a large part, and we extend it by verbal definition to a greater and greater extent as time goes on.[1] Now we are to suppose that one of our conversationalists

[1] Cf. B. Russell, *Human Knowledge: its Scope and Limits*, p. 18.

desires to communicate to the mind of the other some experience of a non-sensory nature (though it may have had sensible concomitants) which has occurred to him. He wants, as he says, to 'share' it with his friend, though, if he is an adherent of the theory which we are now considering, he will hold that the very word 'share' is grossly misleading, since it will be for him a mere matter of definition and logic that an experience cannot be in more than one mind. All that he can hope to do is to give his friend some sort of verbal description by means of which his friend may be able to understand some of the features of the experience which he is describing. (This will be easier if his friend has had a similar kind of experience himself, though, as both the experiences will be *ex hypothesi* non-sensory ones, the difficulty remains as to how they are to be identified through a language constructed out of names of sensible particulars.) Still, he must do his best, and it will be something like this. He will first of all analyse his experience into a number of distinct elements, and in deciding upon the number he will have to strike a middle course between the two extremes. If the number is too small, he will give a grossly over-simplified account of the experience; if it is too large, life will be too short to get the account finished. (This is, in fact, very like the problem of the number of the 'lines' on the television screen; if it is too small the picture will be too crude to give a reasonably accurate impression of the original, but if it is too large the process will become impossibly inconvenient and expensive, and will overcrowd the wave-band.) Then he will have to utter a set of statements which is structurally isomorphic with the experience as thus simplified. The experience is thus coded into words with considerable loss of structure and detail. And then when the message arrives at the eyes or ears of the recipient it will have to be decoded; and this will involve an inevitable loss of clarity owing to the fact that the conversationalists are most unlikely to give precisely the same shades of meaning to their words. It should be added, of course, that the structure which can be communicated may be much more elaborate than the simple grammatical and syntactical structure of the language used; the message may include an indefinitely complicated set of nuances of facial expression, verbal intonation and the like; the essential point, however, is unaltered, that the message must be structurally isomorphic with its intelligible content. Now what I wish to suggest is that this whole picture of human conversation in terms of coding and decoding a message has only a very limited validity. I do not think it is entirely false, and there are situations to which it applies with fair accuracy. Certainly, if I am anxious to transmit to a newspaper the details of an athletic contest or to a business colleague the fluctuations of the stock market, I shall be wise to respect the limitations of information-theory and communication-engineering and not to rely upon the fact that we are two minds with but a single thought, two hearts that beat as one. But as a comprehensive theory of the nature of human intellectual intercourse this view seems to me to suffer from the same fundamental defect as the sensationalist doctrines of perception, namely that they interpret as an *objectum quod* what is really an *objectum quo*. If all communication is of the nature of coding and decoding it is difficult to see how the code can ever have been set up; for even ostensive definition is impossible unless the learner already knows that ostensive definition is what is going on. (It is a well-known fact that a stupid dog will bark at the tip of your finger instead of at the intruder whom you are pointing him to attack.) What, I suggest, needs to be remembered is that language is a means of intercourse between intelligent personal beings; it has an instrumental function which is by no means simply indicated by the extent to which it is structurally isomorphic with the object to which it refers. The whole business of intellectual intercourse is mysterious and complicated to a degree, and one may well despair of doing justice to it by any simple theoretical scheme; the Aristotelians knew this well when they wrote *Mens quodammodo fit omnia*. I argued in a previous chapter that sensible particulars are neither *objecta quae* of perception in which the perceptive act terminates nor are they more or less accurate *copies* of real things; they are *objecta quibus*, media through which the mind acquires a genuine though obscure grasp of the trans-sensory object which is the concrete existent. Now I wish to make a similar assertion about linguistic formulae: that they are neither the *objecta quae* of communication, in which case the conversation would terminate in mere *flatus vocis*, nor are they merely more or less accurate structural replicas of the thought which has been coded into them, but they are *objecta quibus*, means through which two minds are enabled to enter into the sharing of a common intellectual life. This mysterious communion occurs in a baffling variety of ways and at very different levels of mutual interpenetration. Business and scientific English are perhaps its most superficial media; to say this is no disparagement of them, for each can be admirably adapted to its purpose. Intimate conversation, with all that it involves of vocal and facial expression, is ordinarily one of the most profound. But in every case, over and above the mere capacity of language to code information, there is the mutual intercourse of human minds in virtue of which *cor ad cor loquitur*.

If language has this peculiar instrumental capacity, operating on all levels of intimacy and in a vast variety of modes, we ought not to be surprised at the fact that linguistic techniques take extremely different forms according to their subject-matter and their particular function. Furthermore, it must be left to each realm of human thought and life to evolve the technique which is most adequate for its purpose, that which will be most effectual in producing in the mind of the recipient the awareness which the author is endeavouring to bring about. Thus the techniques of poetry, of science, of philosophy, and of theology, will all be different; and indeed in each branch of thought and life there may be a variety of techniques, the excellency of each being judged simply by the extent to which it manages to fulfil its particular function of communication. Nor, in my opinion, ought we to exclude the techniques of art from this function and to suppose that its job is merely to evoke emotion and not, in its own proper way, to communicate truth; I would agree with the late Professor W. G. de Burgh that art is essentially a *cognitive* activity, revealing truth.[1] Nor, again, will music be excluded from this activity of communication, whether we agree to classify it as a form of art or not. These are, however, remarks in passing and do not affect our main theme. It is more to our purpose to point out at this stage that, of all the different types of discourse which the human mind has elaborated that of theology is likely to be one of the most difficult to characterise; for its subject-matter, namely the transcendent God and other beings in their relation to him, stands out in sharp contrast to every other subject of human thought and discourse. We shall go on to discuss its method in some detail, but at the moment I will give two very striking examples which it provides of the way in which a particular discipline may produce a method of communication which is highly singular and indeed at first sight downright bizarre.

[1] Cf. *The Life of Reason*, pp. 60 f.

2. Two Examples of Theological Discourse

It is generally recognised that, of all Christian writers on the excessively difficult subject of mystical theology, the sixteenth-century Spanish mystic St. John of the Cross is the clearest in his grasp of the subject and the most scientific in its treatment. Nobody, I think, could read him with attention without being conscious that he was in the presence of a systematic writer as great in his sphere as St. Thomas Aquinas was in his and without receiving a flood of intellectual enlightenment. But what in fact is St. John's method of writing mystical theology? He first of all writes three poems, the imagery of which is largely taken from the Song of Solomon; as mere poetry these are regarded as among the finest lyrics in the Spanish tongue. Then he writes his treatise on the first stage of the spiritual life as a commentary on the first of these poems, which consists of eight stanzas. However, having expounded two of these stanzas in a little over a fifth of the treatise, he abandons the poem altogether and completes the other four-fifths of the treatise without its aid. Then, in his second treatise, which is concerned with the next stage of the spiritual life, the saint takes up the poem again and commences an exposition of it which differs notably from the previous one. This time he gets as far as the third stanza; what would have happened after that we do not know, as the treatise was left unfinished. Each of the other two poems he expounds at length, devoting a treatise to each, and in each case completing his task. This would indeed seem an unpromising way of writing a scientific account of any subject whatever. Nevertheless, in spite of the artificiality of the technique and the somewhat cavalier way in which it is applied, I do not think anyone could read the Saint's works without being struck by the coherence and profundity of his exposition. One can only suppose that the Carmelite Doctor knew his own business best, and that the apparently unhelpful technique of communication which he employs is in fact extremely well adapted to the nature of the subject-matter with which he is concerned. This does not mean, of course, that it is the only possible technique; other mystical theologians have other ways of going about their business. The point which I am making is simply that every intellectual discipline has its own ways and means and every scholar has his; and their justification is to be found in the extent to which they succeed in their task.

The case which I have just taken is a somewhat extreme one, but I have taken it quite deliberately for that precise reason. For what I wanted to emphasise is that what justifies a particular descriptive technique is not its conformity to a predetermined criterion, but its simple capacity to get its stuff across; there is therefore a real advantage in taking as an example a technique which from almost any conceivable *prima facie* point of view seems quite outlandish and which is nevertheless remarkably successful in performing its task. A more moderate and indeed more typical example is provided by the way in which in dogmatic theology use is frequently made, in expounding some theological truth or mystery, of a number of conceptual or imaginal analogies which if they were applied simultaneously and univocally would be flatly contradictory. I shall give two illustrations of this. The first is concerned with the question whether the Epistle to the Hebrews is consistent with the view that the priesthood of Christ continues throughout the ages or whether it implies that his priesthood came to an end with the Ascension. Protestant controversialists have sometimes argued for the latter view, on the ground that the Epistle declares that our High Priest has sat down on the right hand of the throne of the majesty in the heavens.[1] Now, they point out, the proper posture for a priest is standing, whereas sitting is the proper posture not of a priest but of a king. Furthermore, it is physically impossible for anyone to be sitting and standing at the same time. Hence, they conclude, since Christ is, according to the Epistle, now exercising the functions of a king, he can no longer be exercising the functions of a priest. It will, I think, be clear that the specious validity of this argument depends entirely upon the assumption that both the analogies which are being employed—those of sitting and standing—are to be interpreted as if they were not analogies but univocal descriptions; once this is recognised the argument is seen to be without substance. As Dr. A. M. Ramsey once remarked in my hearing, sitting and standing are indeed incompatible, but the realities which the images of sitting and standing figuratively denote are perfectly compatible all the same. This reply brings out the essential point, but it raises a further question, namely how it is that a figure which is used only analogically manages to describe its object at all. Is not the doctrine of analogy merely a dodge which theologians have adroitly devised in order to get away with downright contradictions?

Before trying to answer this question I shall turn to my second illustration, which I take from the doctrine of redemption and the Atonement. The mystery of the Atonement is generally recognised as one of the most difficult to explain and, in contrast with the mysteries of the Trinity and the Incarnation, there is no one clear-cut doctrine which is generally accepted as the orthodox one. Not only is there nothing precisely like the Atonement—that is true of all the Christian mysteries—but the theologians who have discussed it have made use of a wide variety of picturesque images, which not

[1] Hebrews, viii, 1.

only outsiders but the theologians themselves have commonly regarded as incompatible, so that on this subject Christian theology has tended to split itself up into a number of sharply antagonistic schools. Some theologians have described the atonement as the paying of a bankrupt criminal's fine by a wealthy philanthropist, others as the release of a subject race from the domination of a usurping invader, others again as the healing of a hereditary illness; nor do these three images exhaust the alternatives. Now it is obvious that paying a fine, winning a war and healing a disease are three different activities, which nobody can simultaneously perform. Hence theologians have ranged themselves in mutually opposed groups according to which of the figures they have adopted, and their theories have become correspondingly one-sided and impoverished. If, however, it is recognised that none of the figures applies univocally and with complete adequacy, it will be seen that none of them is to be abandoned, since each of them describes *inadequately* some aspect of the unique mystery. The atonement is something like the paying of a fine, but not entirely so, for the payment of the fine will bring about the prisoner's release irrespective of his personal attitude towards his benefactor. It is something like the release of a captive, but not entirely so, for a man or a people may be in captivity through no fault of their own. It is something like the healing of a disease, but once again there is no moral disgrace in being ill. In fact it is not exactly like anything except itself. Each analogy applies up to a point and no further, the mystery is approached from a number of different directions but each of the approaches stops short, and so there is an insuperable vagueness about its location upon our conceptual map. It lies somewhere within a roughly delimited area, but we cannot say precisely where. Are we to suppose, then, that theological discourse is insuperably imprecise, that it can never lead us to more than approximate knowledge? Not, I think, entirely. To the complete outsider this may very well be more or less the case. The Atonement, he is told, is something like the payment of a fine, but not quite; something like the liberation of an occupied territory, but not quite; something like the curing of an illness, but not quite. What is the unhappy inquirer to make of this object which he is told is to be described by three incompatible comparisons, and by each of them with an undefined margin of error? Very little, no doubt. But it may be sufficient to awaken into consciousness a latent sense of alienation from his true being, and to lead him into the sacramental fellowship of the Church, in which the realities are not only described but experienced. And once a man is inside the Church he will find that the images and figures have a function quite beyond that of describing an unknown object by comparison with objects that are well known: they will, in a strange but unmistakable way, increase his under-standing of a mystery with which he has already begun to be acquainted. They will assist him in that process of pene-tration into the mystery which I described in the last chapter, the process in which an increase of knowledge by acquain-tance goes hand in hand with an enhanced awareness of the extent to which the mystery is still unfathomed. The mystery will now be known obscurely and imperfectly, it is true; but no longer imprecisely. Only in the broadest terms is it possible to indicate the features of this movement of con-templative assimilation of divine truth; for in each of the mysteries it works in a different way and it is in the last resort known not by description but by acquaintance.

Nec lingua potest dicere,
nec littera exprimere;

expertus novit tenere
quid sit Jesum diligere.

To return, then, to our main theme, the assumption that all communication between intelligent beings must depend simply upon the process of coding and decoding, while it has, as I have suggested, its limited validity, is quite inadequate to the facts of experience. 'To us whose intelligence is bound up with language,' writes Professor Susanne Langer, 'whose achievements are physical comforts, machines, medicines, great cities, and the means of their destruction, theory of knowledge means theory of communication, generalisation, proof, in short: critique of science. But the limits of language are not the last limits of experience, and things inaccessible to language may have their own forms of conception, that is to say, their own symbolic devices.'[1] I should not venture to claim Professor Langer's support for all that I have so far said, but this last sentence of hers is, I think, very significant. However, one of the most illuminating expressions that I have found of the thesis which I am maintaining occurs in a small book which is, I think, very little known today but which will lead us on to one of the most important contemporary discussions of theological discourse; this book is the volume on the great Victorian painter G. F. Watts, which was contributed in 1904 by the late Gilbert Keith Chesterton to Messrs. Duckworth's series 'The Popular Library of Art'.

Under the name of 'the infallibility of language' Chesterton attacks what is in essence the doctrine that linguistic communication proceeds simply by the process of coding and decoding. 'Every time one man says to another, "Tell us

---

[1] *Philosophy in a New Key*, p. 265; cit. W. Russell Brain, *Mind, Perception and Science*, p. 88.

24601

plainly what you mean?"', writes Chesterton in the somewhat flamboyant style which was customary with him,

> he is assuming the infallibility of language: that is to say, he is
> assuming that there is a perfect scheme of verbal expression for
> all the internal moods and meanings of men. Whenever a man
> says to another, 'Prove your case; defend your faith,' he is
> assuming the infallibility of language: that is to say, he is
> assuming that a man has a word for every reality in earth, or
> heaven, or hell. He knows that there are in the soul tints more
> bewildering, more numberless and more nameless, than the
> colours of an autumn forest. . . . Yet he seriously believes that
> these things can every one of them, in all their tones and semi-
> tones, in all their blends and unions, be accurately represented
> by an arbitrary system of grunts and squeals. He believes that
> an ordinary civilised stockbroker can really produce out of his
> own inside, noises which denote all the mysteries of memory
> and all the agonies of desire. . . . For the truth is, that language
> is not a scientific thing at all, but wholly an artistic thing, a
> thing invented by hunters, and killers, and such artists, long
> before science was dreamed of.[1]

The only point that I should wish to question in this admirably full-blooded passage—and the point is a purely
verbal one—is the denial of the epithet 'scientific' to language.
In the sense in which Chesterton is using the term, I agree
with him; what he would call the scientific view of language
is what I have described as the doctrine that linguistic communication proceeds simply by coding and decoding. I
would, however, prefer to retain the word 'scientific' if only
on etymological grounds; for since it is the function of
language to communicate knowledge, however mysteri-
ously and obscurely it does this, it seems to me desirable to

[1] Op. cit., p. 88.

make it plain that linguistic discourse is *scientific*, in the sense that it is productive of knowledge.

3. ANALOGY AND ITS JUSTIFICATION

We have, however, by no means disposed of the problem of theological thought and discourse when we have affirmed that linguistic communication involves something more than coding and decoding a message. The fundamental objection still remains, that God is by definition an infinite and supra-sensible being, while all the language that we have in which to talk about him has been devised in order to describe and dis-cuss the finite objects of our sense-experience. How can we use words which signify objects of sensation to talk about an object which has nothing in common with objects of sensa-tion? And how can we use words which signify finite characteristics to talk about an object which is alleged to be unqualifiedly infinite? These are the primary obstacles which any theological system has to face, and we did in fact come straight up against them in the first chapter of this book in relation to Professor Ayer's polemic in *Language, Truth and Logic*. The discussion in that chapter has, I hope, shown that the objections are not unanswerable. It may be well in addition to direct the reader's attention to a number of recent books which have attempted to deal with the question construc-tively. Pride of place should surely be given to Dr. A. M. Farrer's great book *Finite and Infinite*, which was published in 1943. Then there is the late Professor W. G. de Burgh's last book, *The Life of Reason*, which appeared posthumously in 1949. There are a number of books by Roman Catholic writers, notably *The Existence of God* by Dom Mark Ponti-fex and *The Meaning of Existence* by the same author and Dom Illtyd Trethowan; these appeared respectively in 1947

H

and 1953. The last-mentioned writer, who is an example of that unusual figure the avowedly non-Thomist Roman Catholic philosopher, stated his own position at length in 1954, in his *Essay in Christian Philosophy*. I may perhaps be allowed to add that, in a work published in 1949 under the title *Existence and Analogy*, I myself attempted to indicate how the doctrine of analogy was elaborated by the scholastics to deal with precisely the problem which at present concerns us and to show in what way it is capable of development into a form that is relevant to the contemporary situation. There would be little utility in attempting to summarise these various discussions here. It is important, however, to recognise that, in spite of their many differences—for they do not by any means conform to a single pattern—they are alike in not merely admitting the force of the twofold objection mentioned above but in insisting upon it as fundamental to their position. That is to say, it is of the very essence of theism as they see it that God is infinite and supra-sensible: they would repudiate without compromise any suggestion of a God who was merely a magnified version of any or all of the finite beings which are the common objects of our senses. But they would go on to assert that, in spite of this, God can be known and thought and described, however obscurely and imperfectly, on the basis of our experience of the world in which we find ourselves, the world of sensory experience. The grounds on which this assertion can be defended have to some extent been expounded in the first chapter of the present work; for a fuller exposition and argument I must refer the reader to the books which I have named and to others which follow the same general line of thought. Here I shall merely draw attention to three considerations which seem to me to be central to the whole question.

In the first place it must be recognised that the purpose of the doctrine of analogy and similar doctrines is not to prove that it is possible to think and speak about God, but to explain how such a *prima facie* unlikely activity is possible. Against the anti-metaphysical verificationists I would maintain that it is a matter of experience that some people at least sometimes make significant utterances which contain the word 'God' as their subject. Whether anyone has yet produced an entirely satisfactory theory to account for this may be doubted; the classical doctrine of analogy made an attempt to do this, but opinions will no doubt vary about the extent to which it succeeded. My present point is that thought and discourse about God do not have to wait for the elaboration of a watertight explanation of their possibility and their nature. If the doctrine of analogy can provide such an explanation, so much the better for the doctrine of analogy; if it cannot, so much the worse for it, but the activity which it professed to account for will be unscathed. To demand that theological thought and discourse should suspend their operation until an adequate theory about them had been devised would be like arguing that human beings had no right to have children before the rise of the modern science of genetics. It is very important in all these matters to keep the horse in front of the cart.

Secondly, we must recognise that thought about God—knowledge of God—precedes discourse about him. If we could not *know* anything about God, we certainly could not *say* anything about him. And the possibility of knowing God is intimately bound up with the doctrine of creation, that is to say the doctrine about the way in which finite beings are related to him. Now the classical Christian doctrine of creation, while it insists upon a radical difference of nature between God, who is absolutely self-existent, and finite beings, which are altogether dependent upon God, does not

envisage God and creatures as separated by a kind of gulf.[1]
Indeed, the very completeness of the difference of status
between God and finite beings makes the notion of any such
'gulf' entirely inadmissible. For since finite beings are
entirely dependent upon God, they only exist because God is
creatively active at the ontological root of their being, pour-
ing existence into them, as we might say. There is indeed a
strain in modern neo-Protestantism—though there are welcome signs of its dissolution—which postulates between God
and creatures not merely a radical difference of nature and
status but a separation so absolute as to make the creature's
very existence inexplicable and nonsensical. It is not surprising that Dr. Karl Barth's slogan *Finitum non capax infiniti*
went together with a denial not only of the possibility of
natural theology (that is, of any knowledge of God acquir-
able by man's natural powers) but also of any rational understanding of revelation.[2] Such an extreme view is, however,
quite untypical of the historic tradition of Christian
thought, which has recognised that the very insufficiency of
finite beings to maintain themselves involves that God is
intimately present to them and active within them. It is thus
in no way surprising if man is able to acquire a genuine
knowledge of God as the creative ground of the beings which
surround him and of his own self. Admittedly this knowledge will be extremely obscure, for the *quantitative* difference
between God and man (if the term may be allowed) remains
infinite; in his very recognition of God as God, man will
recognise that God exceeds the grasp of both his imagination
and his intellect. There is nothing to puzzle us in the fact that

[1] Cf. my *Existence and Analogy*, ch. vi; *Christian Theology and Natural
Science*, ch. iv. I must, alas, confess to at least a verbal capitulation to the
notion of the 'gulf' in my book *Christ, the Christian and the Church*, p. 92.
[2] Cf. A. M. Farrer, *Finite and Infinite*, p. 2.

we cannot perceive God in the same casual way as we can perceive the Albert Memorial. Nevertheless, the fact remains that God is present as the creative ground of all finite beings. The great book of Dr. Farrer which I have already mentioned, *Finite and Infinite*, provides a masterly discussion of the way in which we can come to recognise this presence, both in other beings and in ourselves, how we can follow both the 'usiological' and the 'anthropological' approach to God. It may be added, though we are not directly concerned with the point at the moment, that it is our complete dependence upon God as our creator that provides the basis in our nature for the possibility of the supernaturalisation of our being which Christian experience knows as the work of grace; only a being which was entirely dependent upon God could have that radical openness to him which Catholic theology describes as the *potentia obedientialis* of nature for the supernatural.[1]

Passing now from our knowledge of God to our speech about God, the third consideration which is, I think, relevant at this point is that, if (as I hold to be the case) it is possible for us, however analogically, to make statements about God by the use of words whose primary application is to the finite beings which we experience through our senses, there must be a certain affinity between God and finite beings which is not excluded by the radical difference which we have seen to characterise their existential status. This has been recognised by traditional Christian philosophy in various ways. In predicating perfections of God, the doctrine of analogy has distinguished between the *perfectio significata*, which is identical in all the analogues, and the *modus significandi* which is determined by the nature of the analogue in each case. Again, it has been asserted that, while it is not strictly correct

[1] This is expounded at greater length in my book *Via Media*, ch. ii and iv.

to say that God is like his creatures, there is a sense in which it must be said that the creatures are like God. Or once again, it has been said that creatures *participate* in God's perfections, while it is made clear that the word 'participate' is not being used in a pantheistic or emanationist sense. This point is not really different from the second one, for, if it is the purpose of language to describe how things are, the relation which holds between God and his creatures on the level of being will be reflected in a relation between the words which are used about God and his creatures on the level of language. Nevertheless, the linguistic consequences merit separate notice, if only for the reason that it does not seem always to be understood how closely linguistics are related to metaphysics.

Perhaps, however, we were really giving our case away when we said just now that the words which we use in order to make statements about God are words whose primary application is to the finite beings which we experience through our senses. *De facto*, this would certainly seem to be true. The word 'powerful' is more likely to evoke in the mind of the modern man the image of a wireless set, a motor car, a bomb, or a political dictator than the concept of Almighty God. The word 'spirit' is more likely to carry associations of motor fuel, alcoholic liquor, or psychological liveliness than of the third Person of the Blessed Trinity. But may this not merely be an indication of the extent to which the mind of the modern man has become secularised? Even when we have made allowance for the fact that *nihil in intellectu quod non fuit prius in sensu*, ought we to say that the application of our words to finite sensible beings is primary *de jure*? Ought we not perhaps rather to say that the two applications, to the finite beings and to God, ideally *go together*? It has often been pointed out that in less sophisticated societies than our own—and this does not necessarily mean less intelligent ones—the normal way of viewing nature was to view it as the creature of God, so that God was directly apprehended as the ground of the world's being and not, as with us, as the final term of a tortuous and questionable chain of argument. Some words of Dr. C. S. Lewis seem to me to be very relevant here. 'Mr. Barfield,' he writes,

has shown, as regards the history of language, that words did not start by referring merely to physical objects and then get extended by metaphor to refer to emotions, mental states and the like. On the contrary, what we now call the 'literal and metaphorical' meanings have both been disengaged by analysis from an ancient unity of meaning which was neither or both. In the same way it is quite erroneous to think that man started with a 'material' God or 'Heaven' and gradually spiritualised them. He could not have started with something 'material' for the 'material', as we understand it, comes to be realised only by contrast to the 'immaterial', and the two sides of the contrast grow at the same speed. He started with something which was neither and both. As long as we are trying to read back into that ancient unity either the one or the other of the two opposites which have since been analysed out of it, we shall misread all early literature and ignore many states of consciousness which we ourselves still from time to time experience. . . .

The Christian doctrines, and even the Jewish doctrines which preceded them, have always been statements about spiritual reality, not specimens of primitive physical science. Whatever is positive in the conception of the spiritual has always been contained in them; it is only its negative aspect (immateriality) which has had to wait for recognition until abstract thought was fully developed.[1]

For examples of the way in which the primitive human mind has manipulated and elaborated its mental images, with

[1] *Miracles*, p. 94.

their peculiar twofold character, we may refer to the chapters on Height, Time, Light and Spirit in the late Dr. Edwyn Bevan's Gifford Lectures on *Symbolism and Belief*. The point which I wish to make here is simply that, in forming concepts and images with this twofold character, primitive man was not manifesting an obstinate disposition to think muddle-headedly, but an implicit grasp of the relation between finite being and its transcendent ground. It is because finite beings participate in the perfection of their Creator and stand in a perpetual relation of dependence upon him as the source from which their existence is derived, that one and the same concept or image can refer both to the Creator and to his creature in different analogical modes. In the *ordo cognoscendi* of secularised man, the order in which his knowledge develops, the finite analogue may indeed come first, and it may be only by a painful process of mental struggle that he comes, if he comes at all, to recognise the transcendent God. But in the *ordo essendi*, the order in which things really are, it is clearly the Creator who comes first, as the source from which everything else proceeds. God is 'the Father from whom all fatherhood in heaven and on earth is named'.[1] And in the *ordo cognoscendi* of unsecularised man, of man who sees finite beings as they really are in their dependence on their Creator and in their participation of his perfection, both the finite and the infinite analogue are given together in the concept or image in their mutual relation. And so it is that, without confusion or ambiguity, the same term can be applied to God and to creatures, the regulative principle of this double use being this, that the difference between the use of the term in its two contexts is based upon, and governed by, the relation of God and creatures in actual concrete reality.

[1] Ephesians, iii, 14.

4. IMAGES AND THEIR PLACE IN THEOLOGY

The theologian is always in some danger of assuming that Christian thought and discourse must be conducted almost entirely in metaphysical terms. It is thus salutary to remind ourselves that the great majority of Christian people are not metaphysicians, and also that the Bible, which is universally accepted by Christians as embodying the revelation of God and as being the source from which Christian theology flows, makes very little use indeed of the language of metaphysics. Its typical instrument of communication is not the concept but the image, and this, as Dr. Farrer among others has pointed out,[1] assimilates the method by which the Bible communicates truths to its readers much more to the method of the poet than to that of the metaphysician. We must therefore inquire in what way human communication relies upon images in doing its work, and I shall resume the discussion from a passage in the book already quoted, in which G. K. Chesterton followed up his attack upon what he called the 'scientific' view of language by an eloquent passage in which, though not perhaps entirely without some confusion of expression, he insisted upon the place that is played in communication by images. 'We can easily imagine an alternative state of things,' he says,

> roughly similar to that produced in Watts' allegories, a system, that is to say, whereby the moods or facts of the human spirit were conveyed by something other than speech, by shapes or colours or some such things. As a matter of fact, of course, there are a great many other languages besides the verbal. Descriptions of spiritual states and mental purposes are conveyed by a variety of things, by hats, by bells, by guns, by fires on a headland or by jerks of the head.[2]

[1] Cf. *The Glass of Vision*, ch. vii.   [2] Op. cit., p. 92.

He goes on—and this is what the discussion is doing in a book on Watts—to point out that one of the great methods of communication is by the use of artistic images, a method in which Watts himself was outstanding. And elsewhere he stresses the fact that, in his choice of images, Watts attempted nothing less than to speak to mankind as a whole.

> In the whole range of Watts' symbolic art there is scarcely a single example of the ordinary and arbitrary current symbol, the ecclesiastical symbol, the heraldic symbol, the national symbol. A primeval vagueness and archaism hangs over all the canvases and cartoons, like frescoes from some prehistoric temple. There is nothing there but the eternal things, clay and fire and the sea, and motherhood and the dead. We cannot imagine the rose or the lion of England; the keys or the tiara of Rome; the red cap of Liberty or the crescent of Islam in a picture by Watts; we cannot imagine the cross itself.[1]

The reason for this policy of iconic self-denial—a policy which, we must note, imposed the most drastic restrictions upon the scope of the artist's imaginative raw material—is almost overwhelming.

> In light and broken phrases, carelessly and humbly expressed, . . . the painter has admitted that this great omission was observed on principle. Its object is that the pictures may be intelligible if they survive the whole modern order. Its object is, that is to say, that if some savage in a dim futurity dug up one of these dark designs on a lonely mountain, though he worshipped strange gods and served laws yet unwritten, it might strike the same message to his soul that it strikes upon clerks and navvies from the walls of the Tate Gallery.[2]

Whether the greatest truths are in fact to be communicated by such a cosmic technique is open to doubt. 'It may plaus-

[1] Ibid., p. 59.   [2] Ibid., p. 60.

ibly be maintained,' wrote Chesterton, 'I am not sure that it cannot more truly be maintained, that man cannot achieve and need not achieve this frantic universality.'[1] Certainly a Christian theologian will feel bound to enter his protest. For all that can be communicated by these universal human images are universal human facts, aspirations, dispositions and characteristics, which are as true of one age as another: Love, Avarice, Hope, Despair, Death, and the like. They are helpless in isolation to declare with the Christian gospel that supreme significance lies in certain particular instances of the great human archetypes: in *this* particular child-bearing of all the millions that have taken place on the earth, in *this* particular human death and not in all the others. Watts could have painted a woman with a child and labelled it 'Motherhood'; he could not without abandoning his canon of universality have placed upon the woman's head a halo with the inscription borne by the Greek icons, *Mētēr Theou*. He could have painted a man hanging upon a cross and entitled it 'Faithful unto death'; he could not consistently have nailed over the head the title *Jesus Nazarenus Rex Judaeorum*. This is a point to which we shall have to return; at the moment I wish rather to emphasise the epistemological character, the function in the process of communication, which can be played by the *image*. No more than in the case of language is it to be understood simply in terms of coding and decoding. There is, of course, a use of images which is simply of this useful and pedestrian type: the employment of a female figure with an anchor to stand for the theological virtue of hope or the equipment of a young girl with a woolly lamb as a more artistic, though perhaps less widely intelligible, method than lettering of indicating that she is St. Agnes. Here, however, we are concerned with something more pro-

[1] Ibid., p. 65.

found than this. There is a whole armoury of images, some of which are limited in their significance to certain communities or groups of people, some of which seem to be the universal possession of the human race as such, whose evocation in the mind has direct epistemological efficacy. To produce a comprehensive psychological theory of the matter is not my purpose here, and it would be extremely difficult in any case; I doubt whether the data have been amassed upon which such a theory might be based. No doubt the followers of Professor C. G. Jung will have valuable contributions to make from their researches into the collective unconscious, whatever the ontological status of the collective unconscious may be. My present point is simply to insist that images, like language, have an epistemological character and function which is not exhausted by description in terms of coding and decoding; the image or the image-complex, like the word or the word-complex, is an *objectum quo*, by the entertainment and contemplation of which the mind is able to enter into intimate cognitive union with the reality of which it is a manifestation.

Before going any further it will, I think, be well to clear up a possible ambiguity. I have spoken a good deal about the epistemological function of the image, and I have related this to the work of the artist as the maker of images *par excellence*. It may seem, however, that I have fallen into confusion between the image, in the sense of the artist's own product—the painting, statue, symphony or poem—and the image in the sense of the 'picture' in the mind of the percipient. I do not think, however, that there is any real ambiguity, for both these 'images' have their part to play in the process by which the artist makes his communication. It is, of course, the mental image—the modification of the percipient's mind—which is the proximate *objectum quo* of the communication. The problem of the artist is how he is to produce this image in the percipient's mind. (I mean, of course, the problem of the artist *in so far as he is trying to communicate*; he may be simply trying to make something which is beautiful, and not to communicate at all, and this is in itself a perfectly respectable and praiseworthy occupation for an artist.) Now the artist's method of producing a mental image is by making a physical image first, by painting a picture or carving a statue, or composing a piece of music or a poem for someone else to perform. From the point of view of communication it is the mental image which matters; everything else is simply instrumental to its production. And it is important to notice that the mental image may be evoked by some other method than by confronting the senses of the beholder with a physical model of it, as for example when we use a word or a phrase which will evoke the image, not by its form, but by its associations or by its descriptive power. I think it is probable that music or poetry acts primarily in this way, in contrast to painting or sculpture. That is to say, the purpose of performing a piece of music or reciting a poem is not primarily to evoke in the hearer's mind an auditory image of the performance, but to arouse certain associated images which will play the main part as *objecta quibus* in the cognitive process. In contrast, the contemplation of a painting or a statue would seem to be primarily concerned to evoke in the beholder's mind an image of the painting or the statue itself, and it will be this image, rather than secondary images associated with it, which will play the part of *objectum quo*. I do not suppose, however, that this contrast between visual and auditory art is anything more than relative; all mental images have other images associated with them, and it is the function of the external physical image to call up these associated images for their role in the cognitive process just as much as to call up the primary mental image which is its replica or 'copy'. The essential element in the process is the production in the percipient's mind of the appropriate images with their instrumental or 'presentative' character as *objecta quibus* for the communication of truth. Attention to a work of art is one way of bringing about this result, but there are others. And we ought to allow for the possibility that there are aspects or regions of reality which can be reached only by the mediation of images or perhaps can only with great difficulty be reached in any other way.

The above is only the barest outline, the merest blueprint, of an epistemology of the image. I can only hope that someone more competent than I will work it out in fuller detail, for it seems to me to be of the greatest importance for the theory of religious knowledge. Traditional Christian Aristotelianism has already a fully worked out doctrine of the epistemological function of the *concept*, as being not merely a picture of the extra-mental object in the manner of the Cartesian *idées-tableaux* but as being a medium through which the object itself is grasped, and indeed as being, in a certain sense, the object itself as grasped by the intellect. The sensory image on the other hand, has too often been seen as a mere impression or copy of the sensible object, with no instrumental function whatever in the cognitive act other than that of being the totally passive material from which the active intellect abstracts an intelligible species. Now I am not arguing for the elaboration of a doctrine of the image and its cognitive role in the sensible order which would be at all points parallel to the accepted doctrine of the concept and its cognitive role in the intellectual order; to do that would be to launch oneself down the slippery slope at the bottom of which lies Locke with his identification of perception with sensation. I am, however, suggesting that we ought to take more seriously the active part which is played by the sensible image in the cognition of reality, and in particular in our cognition of the divine reality from which all other reality draws its being. And part of my reason for this is derived from the central part which images hold in God's revelation of himself in Holy Scripture. It is to this that we must now turn.

In spite of its importance, I shall touch upon this matter only very briefly, for it has been admirably discussed, in a way which limitations of both ability and space prevent my attempting to emulate, by Dr. Farrer in his Bampton Lectures *The Glass of Vision*. The epistemological function which images play in the communication of divine truth is best made plain by the provision of examples; Farrer has followed this course to some extent in the lectures just mentioned, and notably in the glowing passage in which he displays the monumental way in which the New Testament amasses and interlocks the great images which it uses to declare the mystery of the Holy Trinity. A more extended application of his method is given in his books on the New Testament itself, and notably in the great work on the Apocalypse of St. John which is entitled *A Rebirth of Images*. Farrer is insistent that the images cannot fulfil their proper epistemological function if they are approached in a merely rationalistic spirit. 'It is surely of high importance,' he writes,

to know what is to be looked for in Scripture. The Medieval Scholastic mind, it would seem, was (in theory at any rate) on the hunt for theological propositions, out of which a correct system of doctrine could be deduced by logical method. If we set about the quest in that way, we close our ears to the voice of Scripture. The modern tendency is to seek after historical record, whether it be the record of events, or of spiritual states in apostolic minds: it is not surprising if it fails to find either the voice of God, or the substance of supernatural mystery. We have to listen to the Spirit speaking divine things: and the way to appreciate his speech is to quicken our own minds with the life of the inspired images.[1]

Amusingly stigmatising what he describes as the method of the research degree, which attempts to interpret the mind of a Biblical writer by a statistical and lexicographical analysis of his text and to 'draw into the light the system which was coming to birth in the Apostle's mind', Farrer goes on as follows:

> But suppose there was no system coming to birth in the Apostle's mind at all—not, that is, on the conceptual level? Suppose that his thought centred round a number of vital images, which lived with the life of images, not of concepts. Then each image will have its own conceptual conventions, proper to the figure it embodies: and a single over-all conceptual analysis will be about as useful for the interpretation of the Apostle's writings as a bulldozer for the cultivation of a miniature landscape-garden. The various images are not, of course, unconnected in the Apostle's mind, they attract one another and tend to fuse, but they have their own way of doing this, according to their own imagery laws, and not according to the principles of conceptual system.[2]

It is an essential point in Farrer's position that for the understanding of the images it is not necessary for us to get behind them to a non-metaphorical understanding of fact. The images themselves illuminate us.[3] He admits that at first sight such an assertion will seem logically scandalous, but he supports it by drawing a parallel from the method of analogy in metaphysics. He summarises his argument as follows:

> What was puzzling us was the function of images in revealed truth. The scandal appeared to be, that we cannot point away from the revealed images to any imageless or 'straight' truth

<hr>

[1] *The Glass of Vision*, p. 44.   [2] Ibid., p. 45.   [3] Ibid., p. 62.

which the images signify. So we decided to consider the use of images outside the special province of revealed truth, and took up the broader province of metaphysics. Well, and what have we discovered? Can the metaphysician point away from the analogical statements he uses to a non-analogical truth which they state? We cannot answer yes or no to that: the question is ambiguous: the reply depends on what you mean by the non-analogical *truth*. If by truth you mean a piece of true *thinking*, the answer is No: the metaphysician cannot point away from his analogically expressed thoughts about the natural mysteries to some non-analogical thoughts about them, which mean all that the analogical thoughts mean. He has not got any such non-analogical thoughts: analogy is the proper form of metaphysical thought, in the realm of *thought* there is no getting behind it.

If, on the other hand, by 'truth' you mean the existent reality which the metaphysician is talking about, then indeed he can in a sense point to a truth outside his analogical statements, which they are designed to state. For he can point to the natural mysteries. Without analogising he can do no more than point to them, or at the most name them: he cannot express or describe them. He can, without analogising, say 'There is what I call myself, and there is what I call my body, and the two have something to do with one another.' But what it is they have to do with one another can only be stated in analogies.[1]

In Farrer's view, the ordinary healthy thinking, of which metaphysics is the systematic elaboration, is simply contemplation; this, of course, links up with one of the main contentions of my last chapter.

Get a man to see the mysterious depth and seriousness of the act by which he and his neighbour exist, and he will have his eyes turned upon the bush in which the supernatural fire

[1] *The Glass of Vision*, p. 73.

I

appears, and presently he will be prostrating himself with Moses, before him who thus names himself: 'I am that I am.'[1]

Farrer holds that there is a definite parallel between the way in which the contemplative metaphysical approach to the natural mysteries can lead by an analogical passage to the God who is nature's creator and the way in which by living with and feeding upon the great revealed images of the Bible we can be led to knowledge of the supernatural mysteries of the Christian Faith. 'Nevertheless,' he tells us,

> rational analogies and revealed images concerning God do not function in the same way: and we can express the difference by saying that the rational analogies are *natural* images: the revealed figures are not, in the sense intended, *natural.*
>
> The rational analogies are natural, first of all, in the sense that they may be, and originally are, spontaneous: unless finite things put themselves upon us as symbols of deity we can have no natural knowledge of God. Revealed images do not do this: they are authoritatively communicated. The stars may seem to speak of a maker, the moral sense of a law-giver: but there is no pattern of being we simply meet, which speaks of Trinity in the Godhead or the efficacy of the Sacraments. . . .
>
> Rational analogies are natural in a second sense: the analogy which the natural symbol appears to bear to God is founded on a real relation in which it stands towards God. Suppose, for example, I take my will as a symbol of God, because it seems to be a limited instance of something intrinsically infinite, sheer creativity. In such a case the symbolical relation corresponds with a real relation: . . . my will symbolises God because it participates of God. Whereas revealed images are commonly just parables. For example, I am taught the mystery of Christ's mystical body in terms of physical organism. But there is no real and causal relation between natural organisms and Christ's mystical body: bodies, by being bodies, do not really par-

[1] Ibid., p. 78.

ticipate in the mystery of saving incorporation. I do in fact participate in Christ's mystical body, but not by being a natural bodily creature: I participate in Christ's body by a supernatural and imperceptible gift; and this gift is no part of the figure by which revelation teaches me about the body of Christ. . . . Only the figures are revealed, and the figures are simply parables.[1]

Thus, for Farrer, the images through which the Christian revelation is mediated to us do not function simply in virtue of their iconic character, simply by being the sort of images they are, in such a way that they would carry their message to any human being in any age who happened to stumble upon them. Their efficacy does not depend simply upon the natural power of the human mind to recognise likenesses, to abstract universals from particulars, to 'put things together and take them apart', as Aristotle says. The images were provided by God to his ancient people the Jews in the Old Testament revelation, they were taken by Christ and refashioned and synthetised, and this work continues in the Apostles and the Church.

It was possible for Christ and the Apostles to use the images meaningfully, because the old archetypes were there to hand, already half transformed under the leading of God in the expectant faith of Israel. Christ clothed himself in the archetypal images, and then began to do and to suffer. The images were further transformed by what Christ suffered and did when he had put them on: they were transformed also by their all being combined in his one person. . . .

The choice, use and combination of images made by Christ and the Spirit must be simply a supernatural work: otherwise Christianity is an illusion. . . .

The images are supernaturally formed, and supernaturally made intelligible to faith. Faith discerns not the images, but

[1] Ibid., p. 94.

what the images signify: and yet we cannot discern it except *through* the images. We cannot by-pass the images to seize an imageless truth.[1]

Thus the images are divinely selected and divinely arranged before they are presented to us as the *objecta quibus*, through which we can apprehend the divine realities, the *objecta quae*. But even when the images have been presented to us we cannot perceive the divine realities by our own natural powers. It is faith, and not natural reason, which is the *lumen sub quo* of our supernatural knowledge; and faith is our response to the revealing activity of God. Thus Dr. Farrer, in his epistemology of the supernaturally given image, draws together all the threads of Catholic doctrine. The supernatural mystery, the divinely provided medium, the elevation of grace, the appropriation of divine life in contemplation, all these are brought together in a profound and coherent synthesis; and in this the *image*, as God's chosen means of speaking to man, occupies the central place.

[1] Ibid., pp. 109–110.

VI

CONCLUSION

THROUGHOUT this book we have been concerned with one central task, that of providing a rational justification for the activities of thinking and talking about God, both as he is in himself and as he is manifested in his dealings with us. In doing this, I found it necessary to begin by examining certain widely publicised positions, which if accepted would dismiss our task as irrelevant and doomed to futility from the start. The upshot of this examination was that there appeared to be no valid reasons for accepting these positions, and I suggested that their fundamental weakness lay in an uncritical assumption that perception is essentially identical with sensation, as a result of which our knowledge of the world was arbitrarily blocked at the level of sensible phenomena. Against this view I argued that perception is primarily an *intellectual act*, an act in which the mind utilises the phenomenon as an *objectum quo* and passes through it to grasp the concrete trans-sensible reality, whose nature is that not of sensible but of intelligible being. I asserted that only in this way was it possible to maintain, not only that we can come to know and to speak about God as the creative ground of the universe, but also that we can come to know and speak about physical objects and persons other than our own selves. I was then led to criticise the ideal of the cognitive process which, on the basis of its remarkable success in an important but very limited field of experience, has been extended by the dominant school of modern Anglo-Saxon philosophy to cover experience as a whole, that is to say, the ideal of knowledge as detached, discursive and arrested at the level of phenomena; and I suggested that the driving force behind this movement has been an over-anxious determination to avoid the possibility of error even at the expense of a quite ruthless impoverishment of the range of human knowledge. Over against this I set another ideal of knowledge as involving commitment, contemplation and penetration beneath the phenomenal level, and I pointed out that, by the nature of the case, it is only by such an approach to them that the realities with which Christianity is concerned can be discovered and explored. Then, in my last chapter, I raised the question of the relation of theological thought and knowledge to its communication, and here we saw that, while, like other branches of human activity, theology and religion make widespread use of concepts, they are specially involved in the use of images, if only for the very sufficient reason that images are the means that God himself has chosen in order to reveal his own thoughts to men. Here I found myself greatly in debt to the admirable investigations which Dr. Farrer has made into this question.

My hope, as I come to the end of my argument, is that I have done something to show that the discourse of Christian theology and religion is neither psittacistic nonsense nor disguised pep-talk, but is rational conversation, albeit rational conversation of a unique type which has its own peculiar method and discipline. If I have been successful in this task the way should now lie open for the application of its principles to the specific questions with which theology is concerned; I shall resist the temptation to enter upon this here, for it would involve nothing less than a survey of the whole field of dogmatic theology. For a specific example of a theological discussion which at least attempts to conform to our requirements and to avoid mere verbalism on the one hand and phenomenalistic positivism on the other—which tries, that is, to submit itself to being governed and controlled by the concrete object with which it is concerned—I may perhaps refer to a small book called *Via Media*, in which I have attempted to apply systematically a fundamental theological principle to the four mysteries of Creation, the Trinity, the Incarnation and Grace. Here I shall simply conclude the present discussion by giving a very brief indication of one way in which analogical thought can operate upon the two basic dogmas of the Christian revelation. These two dogmas are that, in God, three Persons, Father, Son and Spirit, are united in one divine essence or nature, and that, in Jesus of Nazareth, two natures, a human and a divine, are united in one divine Person. All the terms which occur in these formulations, with one exception, are derived from our experience of the sensible world in which we live: 'father', 'son' and 'spirit' (that is, in the classical languages of Christian theology, 'wind' or 'breath') are the names of perceptible physical objects; 'person', 'nature', 'human' and even 'divine' are words used in common speech, and 'Jesus of Nazareth' is the name of a historical human individual, who taught and was crucified in Palestine in the procuratorship of Pontius Pilate. Only the word 'God' stands apart as the name of a transcendent super-sensible being; but as the first of our two formulations claims to give a description of God he too is assimilated by it to the objects of ordinary experience. Even the small word 'in' has a meaning that is commonplace and spatial; business men sit 'in' their offices, and housewives put joints 'in' ovens. What, then, are we doing when we say that 'in' God there are three Persons 'in' one nature, or that 'in' Jesus there are two natures 'in' one

Person? That the three Persons are in the one nature as the
business man is in his office? That the two natures are in the
one Person like the joint in the oven? Clearly not. Well, it
may be said, even in ordinary speech, 'in' is often used meta-
phorically and not in its primary spatial sense: Selwyn
Lloyd is in the Government, for example, or the man who
was caught driving without a licence is in hot water. Will
either of these uses help? Hardly at all, alas; and once we get
away from the primary meaning into the secondary ones,
there is the added trouble that, while the secondary meanings
all bear *some* relation to the primary one, they usually bear
much less relation to one another. If we are going to be
guided by ordinary uses, it may even be less misleading
(*salva reverentia*) to think of the relation of the divine person
to the two natures as being like the relation of the oven to the
joint than as being like the relation of the hot water to the
motoring offender. Clearly there is no way out along this
road; and even when the doctrine of analogy has done
for us all that it can in providing us with a common *perfectio
significata* we shall still not know where to look for our
modus significandi. It is, however, at this point that we must
remember that theological concepts and images do not come
to us *in vacuo*; as Dr. Farrer has done so great a service in
reminding us, they are given to us in the divinely provided
context of the Judaeo-Christian revelation, bearing with them
the manifold overtones and associations with which God has
equipped them, and they come to us as members of the body
of Christ, to which God has committed the Spirit of understanding. This does not detach them from their roots in the
everyday world of the senses, for God is the sovereign of the
natural order as well as the order of grace: 'the Most High
hath not made one world, but two.'[1] It is this organic con-

[1] II Esdras vii [50].

nection between the two orders that can preserve the thought of the Christian on the one hand from the naturalism which would interpret the concepts and images of the Bible and Christian theology in the grossest univocal way ('the manhood is in the divine Son like the joint in the oven') and on the other hand from a sheer verbalism which would detach them from their roots in ordinary life altogether and turn the statements of theology into uncontrolled ecstatic babblings. From neither of these temptations is the Christian free, and the history of the Church offers sad examples of submission to both of them; perhaps at no time have they been altogether evaded. Nevertheless in the Sacred Scriptures we see how God has chosen and moulded the great images, which Christ combined and fulfilled and fashioned to be his own garment; and in the Church which is Christ's body we see these same images, not running wild in ungoverned proliferation but controlled by the indwelling Spirit who both guides their own growth and gives to men who have faith and humility the eyes and ears to understand them. Thus, in the last resort, we cannot understand the nature of Christian thought and discourse by simply formulating a theory about it, correct though such a theory may be, but only by contemplating it patiently and reverently in the life of the Christian Church. For, rooted though it is in the natural order, wherein the Word of God is the light that lighteth every man, it can only be understood in its fulfilment in Christ, the Word who is made flesh and dwells with us. Christian thought is not an activity which is open to any man at any time who is prepared to practise it diligently and apply the proper principles of procedure: it is an activity of the Body of Christ, initiated by the Incarnate Word in the days of his flesh and continued by him in his body the Church under the control of the indwelling Spirit. Like all his other activities in his mystical body, it is hampered by the blindness and distorted by the wilfulness of his members; but it remains his activity. It is God who gives the great images to the Church, and God by whose indwelling activity the Church is enabled to interpret them: and it is by his indwelling activity in their souls that men are able to understand the Church's voice. Here indeed we see as in a glass darkly, and not yet face to face; nevertheless we see. And in our thought and speech about him as in all else, God does not destroy the powers of our nature but confirms them and validates them, even in the act by which he makes them the raw material of supernature and grace.

BIBLIOGRAPHY

AYER, A. J., *The Foundations of Empirical Knowledge*. London: Macmillan, 1940.

——, *Language, Truth and Logic*. London: Gollancz. 2nd ed., 1946.

——, *Philosophical Essays*. London: Macmillan, 1954.

——, *The Problem of Knowledge*. London: Penguin Books, 1956.

AYER, A. J., and others, *The Revolution in Philosophy*. London: Macmillan, 1956.

BARTSCH, H. W. (editor), *Kerygma and Myth. A Theological Debate*. London: S.P.C.K., 1953.

BENEDICTINE OF STANBROOK, A., *Medieval Mystical Tradition and St John of the Cross*. London: Burns Oates, 1954.

BEVAN, E., *Symbolism and Belief*. London: Allen and Unwin, 1938.

BRAIN, W. RUSSELL, *Mind, Perception and Science*. Oxford, Blackwell, 1951.

BRAITHWAITE, R. B., *Scientific Explanation*. Cambridge University Press, 1953.

——, *An Empiricist's View of the Nature of Religious Belief*. Cambridge University Press, 1955.

BROAD, C. D., *Religion, Philosophy and Psychical Research*, London: Routledge, 1953.

BURTT, E. A., *The Metaphysical Foundations of Modern Physical Science*. London: Routledge. 2nd ed., 1932.

CHESTERTON, G. K., *G. F. Watts*. London: Duckworth, 1904.

——, *Collected Poems*. London: Burns Oates, n.d.

DE BURGH, W. G., *The Life of Reason*. London: Macdonald and Evans, 1949.

FARRER, A. M., *Finite and Infinite*. London: Dacre Press, 1943.

——, *The Glass of Vision*. London: Dacre Press, 1948.

FARRER, A. M., *A Rebirth of Images*. London: Dacre Press, 1949.

FLEW, A. G. N. (editor), *Logic and Language*. Oxford: Blackwell. First Series, 1951.

FLEW, A. G. N., and MACINTYRE, A. (editors), *New Essays in Philosophical Theology*. London: S.C.M., 1955.

GUIBERT, J. DE, *The Theology of the Spiritual Life*. London: Sheed and Ward, 1954.

LANGER, S. K., *Philosophy in a New Key*. Cambridge (Mass.): Harvard University Press, 1942.

LASLETT, P. (editor), *The Physical Basis of Mind*. Oxford: Blackwell, 1950.

LEWIS, C. S., *Miracles*. London: Bles, 1947.

MARITAIN, J., *Distinguer pour unir: Les Degrés du Savoir*. Paris: Desclée. 2nd ed., 1932.

MASCALL, E. L., *He Who Is. A Study in Traditional Theism*. London: Longmans, 1943.

——, *Christ, the Christian and the Church*. London: Longmans, 1946.

——, *Existence and Analogy*. London: Longmans, 1949.

——, *Christian Theology and Natural Science*. London: Longmans, 1956.

——, *Via Media. An Essay in Theological Synthesis*. London: Longmans, 1956.

MOORE, G. E., *Philosophical Studies*. London: Kegan Paul, 1922.

PATON, H. J., *The Modern Predicament*. London: Allen and Unwin, 1955.

PIEPER, J., *Leisure the Basis of Culture*. London: Faber, 1952.

PONTIFEX, M., *The Existence of God*. London: Longmans, 1947.

PONTIFEX, M., and TRETHOWAN, I., *The Meaning of Existence*. London: Longmans, 1953.

PRICE, H. H., *Perception*. London: Methuen, 1932.

RUSSELL, B. (Earl), *An Introduction to Mathematical Philosophy*. London: Allen and Unwin. 2nd ed., 1920.

——, *Our Knowledge of the External World*. London: Allen and Unwin. 2nd ed., 1926.

——, *An Outline of Philosophy*. London: Allen and Unwin, 1927.

RUSSELL, B. (Earl), *Human Knowledge: its Scope and Limits*. London: Allen and Unwin, 1948.

SPENS, W., *Belief and Practice*. London: Longmans, 1917.

TOULMIN, S., *The Philosophy of Science*. London: Hutchinsons, 1953.

TRETHOWAN, I., *An Essay in Christian Philosophy*. London: Longmans, 1954.

URMSON, J. O., *Philosophical Analysis: its Development between the two World Wars*. Oxford University Press, 1956.

WHITE, V., *God the Unknown*. London: Harvill, 1956.

WHITEHEAD, A. N., *Symbolism, its Meaning and Effect*. Cambridge University Press, 1928.

——, *Process and Reality. An Essay in Cosmology*. Cambridge University Press, 1929.

WILLIAMS, C., *The Place of the Lion*. London: Gollancz, 1931.

——, *Descent into Hell*. London: Faber, 1937.

WISDOM, JOHN, *Philosophy and Psychoanalysis*. Oxford: Blackwell, 1953.

WISDOM, J. O., *The Metamorphosis of Philosophy*. Cairo: Al-Maaref Press, 1947.

WITTGENSTEIN, L., *Tractatus Logico-Philosophicus*. London: Routledge, 2nd ed., 1933.

——, *Philosophical Investigations*. Oxford: Blackwell, 1953.

INDEX OF PROPER NAMES

Date Due